HUGHIE GRIFFITHS was born in 1931, fifth in a family of seven, on a small hill farm on the Herefordshire/Wales border. With school masters called up, his 'education' consisted mainly of working on the home farm and cultivating the school gardens, leaving at fourteen with 'Retarded' on his school report. Then, at the age of thirty-one, following gardening jobs, military service and various retail jobs, and with family commitments, he settled for manual factory work.

With settled home life and working hours, he began to catch up on his missed wartime education. After Craft Certificates, he passed his first (of eleven) O level at thirty-three and obtained an Open University Degree at forty-five in 1976. That same year, he was elected onto Warwick District Council, representing a Leamington Ward, which included five-, eight-, and fourteen-storey blocks of flats. Contrary to his expectations, he found his Council duties very daunting. Read on…

So You're One of our Idle Councillors?

Seven Years a District Councillor
1976–1983

So You're One of our Idle Councillors?
Seven Years a District Councillor 1976–1983

Hughie Griffiths

ATHENA PRESS
LONDON

So You're One of our Idle Councillors?
Seven Years a District Councillor, 1976–1983
Copyright © Hughie Griffiths 2009

All Rights Reserved

ISBN 978 1 84748 609 7

First published 2009 by
ATHENA PRESS
Queen's House, 2 Holly Road
Twickenham TW1 4EG
United Kingdom

Printed for Athena Press

Author's Note

I wish to point out that this book was written in 1984 but not published until 2009, therefore some references may be dated. I apologise for any ambiguity resulting from this passage of time, however these were my experiences of public life during the seven-year period 1976–1983 written when they were fresh in my mind.

Contents

Introduction	11
Public Inquiry	13
Council Meetings and Group Meetings	17
Membership of Outside Bodies	27
Councillors' 'Surgeries'	40
Dealing with the Press	55
Studies	65
Councillor's Allowances and Family Involvement	75
Time-off-work Problems	95
Of Clerks, Cabbages and Cockerels	112
Knees-up on the Rates	130
Try for Parliament	145
Fan Mail	149

Introduction

I was not to know it but the Parliamentary Selection Conference to choose Labour's candidate for the Warwick and Leamington Constituency was to be virtually the end of my political 'career'. The very next evening I failed reselection for a chance to stand again in the Ward that I had represented on the District Council for six and a half years – having topped the poll at the two previous elections.

It all made headline stories in the local provincial town press: 'Labour stalwart's double setback' the *Coventry Evening Telegraph* billed it.

The non-selection as a Parliamentary Candidate was no surprise to anyone. I was just trying my arm as it were. Riding the crest of a popularity wave – why not give it a try? No harm could be done and it would be a further experience to look back on in later years.

Clang!

Once you are marked down as a loser in politics the whole pack of cards collapses. The next night I was out of my District Council Ward as well, an untried new member having been picked instead to stand at the forthcoming local elections.

On polling day my 600 majority was swept away and Labour lost a safe seat to the Tories. I shall never understand why I tumbled from favour so completely in the space of two days after six and a half years as a prominent District Councillor – but that's politics. This book is that six-and-a-half-year story, plus the remaining six months I served out to finish my term in office, i.e. seven years as a District Councillor – 1976–1983.

I had put everything into representing the Ward on the Council – on School Boards and Outside Bodies including the Youth Centre, Marriage Guidance Council, Warwickshire Environmental Protection Council and Community Health Council. I had become well known for taking up individual constituents' complaints. I had assisted their collective battles against the problems of high-rise flats, dampness, mould, high electricity bills, inferior road surfaces, refuse collections, grass cutting and dog nuisances of one sort and another.

I had maintained contact with the Party, attending regular Branch/Group/Constituency meetings. Indeed at one time or another I had held most offices – Branch Chairman, Constituency Treasurer, Temporary Group Secretary, Temporary Branch Secretary, Branch Treasurer – a regular dogsbody in fact. Yet I was not reselected to stand a third time as District Councillor. Small hope of getting the Parliamentary selection; but I had been shortlisted four times during that Parliamentary campaign.

Such is politics. However, I saw it then and now as trying to help my neighbours and workmates. It was linking up with neighbours and workmates in the form of fellow allotmentors in an effort to prevent an allotment site being developed that started it all off.

Public Inquiry

We lived in a house that was the last one in a cul-de-sac, but a farm drive continued to Stud Farm. Quite famous horses had been born there including an Epsom winner, April the Fifth and ESB (ESB, Epsom-trained, raced past the prostrate Devon Lock in a memorable Grand National), hence the road was called Epsom Road. However, all good things come to an end and in 1970 the last seventeen acres of Stud Farm were sold for £72,000 an acre to a Developer. That sort of money is very tempting even to the most entrenched owners. Thus the owner of a two-to-three-acre adjoining allotment site, trapped between these seventeen acres and the main road, also sold out. The allotment site became the subject of a Public Inquiry. The District Council, with the allotmentors and local people, were on the one side wishing to retain it for environmental/amenity reasons, and the Developer (complete with Queen's Counsel) was on the other side. He wished to develop the area as a 'package' with his seventeen acres behind it.

I worked two allotments, but not on this site. However, as Secretary/Treasurer of my site I had fought off biannual attempts over the previous fifteen years or so by the very same District Council (now on our side), to build houses, schools, a fire station, water reservoir and a through road – every twist in the book in fact. Eventually, in order to negotiate from strength, I had formed the eleven local Allotment Associations into an Allotment Council, affiliated to the National Allotment body and thus found myself speaking at the Public Inquiry – defending allotmentor's rights. (Subsequently I was co-opted on to the Local Council's Allotment Committee).

The site had been allotments since 1751 – over 200 years – and was fully let. It would be needed as a 'breathing lung' in the built-up areas – last sanctuary for birds, wildlife, insects and butterflies. It was also needed to protect very old fruit trees and established hedgerows which were amenities in themselves; above all else the fruit and vegetables supplemented low incomes, pensions and unemployment benefits. Also the site was an escape to otherwise house-trapped pensioners and their like. All of this was expanded into a three-page submission for the Public Inquiry and is now lodged with that allotment site's records in Warwick Records Office for posterity to ponder.

When the government-appointed Inspector realised five members of the public wished to speak at 'his' Public Inquiry, he interrupted proceedings with a, 'Couldn't one of you speak for all five? I have to be in Oxford by tomorrow' – very curtly stated as if we were taking a liberty.

The time was only about 11.30 a.m. and Oxford is only a shopping trip away from Leamington Spa. He was on an expenses-paid tour anyway, so where was the problem? On top of that he placed no such curb on the five-man Developer's team.

My disillusionment in 'Public' Inquires was instant and rapidly deepened when he refused a Council Officer's request to break for lunch, stating, 'I'm completing this Inquiry first' – and he did.

The Warwick District Officers, thinking pre-lunch submissions would be only at a preliminary level had not brought with them some ninety letters of protest from the public. He ruled them out as inadmissible despite officers offering to go for them (in the same Town Hall building) because they were not to hand, i.e. his hand, he explained.

I had informed neighbours, friends and fellow allotmentors (via notices on the allotments noticeboards) to make their presence felt by arriving after lunch – thus they would not disrupt their day needlessly. They duly arrived – and missed the 'Public' Inquiry!

From this experience of local government and Westminster Government at work, I was determined to take a more active part before it was too late and Government-by-negligence and/or decree became standard.

The total lack of any elected representatives at the Public Inquiry stood out a mile. I did not realise at that time that Constituents had to lobby them before they took an interest (in the main). Naively I thought that was incumbent upon them once they were elected. The problems of their work and family/home commitments never entered my head either – I was, of course, a normal member of the undiscerning public, believing Councillors had nothing else to do.

Within a very short space of time this same Developer opened up the narrow cul-de-sac in front of my house in Epsom Road and started building. Thus I was immediately into another battle – the right to live in a cul-de-sac in accordance with the situation when the houses were bought, having paid solicitor's search fees to establish the fact.

This time I was not representing an organisation. Also the protesting public were few in number because there were only twelve houses in the cul-de-sac. In order to maximise our protest I drew up a petition. Even so, it needed a Councillor to present it for maximum effect in the District Council meeting.

Thus it was I first contacted my local Labour District Councillor, joined the Party, got even deeper involved in local politics, until just four years later I stood and was elected as a Labour District Councillor. I topped the poll in my first attempt despite running alongside two existing Councillors in the Ward.

The battle to re-close Epsom Road still continues although I have moved away in the meantime, heading towards fields again, no doubt to witness the same problems all in due course.

Being elected onto the very District Council that wished to develop 'my' allotment site prevented me from continuing that fight. I had to declare an interest in Council each time the issue came up. They too were developed by the Council for houses just five years later. Therefore, despite the local press greeting my election with 'The surprising success of the local allotment organiser', I could only say, 'Declare an interest, Mr Chairman' on the subject thereafter. Most other Councillors' particular areas of expertise are buried in the same way also.

I had taken the plots on when I married, gardened them for twenty-six years and been Secretary/Treasurer of the site for eighteen years. You do not just lose fruit and vegetables, but also a chunk (your chunk) of the countryside – the four seasons, birds, bees the lot – but above all else you lose the company. As a non-smoker and non-drinker, I enjoyed the company on the allotments, exchanged gardening and working jokes and stories, kept in touch with work and learnt about short time and lay-offs in other factories in the area, watched mates' children go from toddlers to nuisances to helpers – to young people with girl- or boyfriends – in leaps of one or two yearly intervals depending on how much they liked to 'help' dad on the allotment.

I miss my allotments, but I was by now on the District Council and there were other things to attend to.

Council Meetings and Group Meetings

After I had stood and been elected on a 'Party ticket' the first meeting needing my attendance was the Party Group meeting, i.e. the elected group of Labour Councillors meeting in advance of the Council's Annual General Meeting which always follows an election – pronto.

The Labour Group made up only a quarter of the Council but nevertheless was by far the second-largest group – hence we were 'The Opposition' as it were. As such, Group meetings were always serious affairs with a strict order of business. The first meeting automatically became the Group's Annual General Meeting where Group Officers were elected for the year, and other posts were filled, as we shall now see.

We were all Party activists and therefore knew one another's capabilities, past record, commitments and family ties, thus Group Officers (Group Leader, Deputy Group Leader and Group Secretary) selected themselves in effect; no challenge was put to names put forward by established Councillors. (No Treasurer was needed since no money was involved.) We then proceeded along the same lines to select Shadow Chairmen of the Main Committees, and hence to select which Committee the rest of us would serve on.

It worked out at four Committees each, assuming we would be able to reflect our full strength on each Committee. (Controlling Groups do not always allow this, especially where they are only marginally in command of the Council). This exercise turned out to be much more difficult than just balancing members' interests with appropriate Committees, i.e. housing specialists on Housing Committee, planning experts on Plans, etc., with also-rans filling in remaining vacancies.

Every newly elected Labour Councillor thinks his Ward has the biggest housing problems – bearing in mind that Labour Councillors were returned almost exclusively in urban Wards. Second, no one wants the Cinderella Committees where they will not be noticed, for example Environmental Health (at that time – now it is a much more prominent topic). Also because Warwick District has three main towns in its area, Housing (for example) needed a Councillor from each of the three towns. Ditto for Plans Committee. Rapidly members' special interests and talents take second place. For example, one from each town on Housing left only one more place to be filled – and all eleven other Councillors thought they qualified to fill it.

It was news to me that an elected member could not turn up on any Committee even if he could not vote. You attend the Committees you are selected on to (if confirmed at the forthcoming AGM of the Council) and that's your lot – by order of the Controlling Group.

I was to smash that dictate within a few months of being elected and, after much consternation, the Tories gave way in the face of bad publicity.

After Shadow Chairmen, the three town representation and some obvious leading members' special talents were accommodated, the shuffling for the remaining places on Committees left several newly elected members very disappointed. It is my opinion one or two (only) never readjusted to this secondary role after the euphoria of being selected, canvassing and being elected. Given the subsequent rough and tumble of politics in general once you have declared your colour, they never surfaced as speech makers in the actual Council Chamber. It was not unknown for some not to turn up after having received a 'bloody nose' when trying to make a point or ask a question in Council. More of maiden speeches later, when you will see what I mean by 'bloody nose'.

At last the Group settled who was on which Council Committee and agreed the list to be forwarded to the Controlling Group for their approval (or otherwise) before its formal ratification at the full Council's AGM.

Along the way during this selection process in the Group, newly elected members checked out issues on which they had to declare an interest each time the subject came up for discussion. In those days council-house tenants could not speak or vote on council house issues, because directly or indirectly it affected the amount of rent they paid or would subsequently pay. This was an odd situation because most council-house tenants voted at Elections for one of their fellow tenants, if possible, in order to get Councillors with first-hand experience of their problems. The Secretary of State has now released such Councillors to do just that – but not where levels of rents are directly involved. That is still taboo.

Many Councillors with inside knowledge of a subject are ruled out of discussions on this basis, e.g. builders from building contracts (a minefield of hidden snags to the uninitiated), farmers from farming problems such as stubble-burning pros and cons, and so on, hence I could no longer fight for my allotment site.

However, for now, back to the first Group Meeting.

Following the Committee selections and advice to new members (over quite quickly in practice) there followed a most remarkable 'cattle market' period which took me completely by surprise, and which I still question from an ethical point of view. But it still happens all over the country.

'School Governorships!' the Group Leader (Chair) called, and thereupon proceeded down a list of twenty-nine schools, Special Schools plus colleges. From time to time he stopped as a member claimed a place on the Board of this or that school.

I was left aghast and, temporarily, without any School Governorship, not having made a bid during the procedure.

School Governors, or School Managers in my day, had always been personages revered by me. I had no idea such places were grabbed as at a jumble sale. However, long before the Group Leader had completed going through the list, shouts of 'Mine' had dried up. Members now accepted a Governorship reluctantly – even refused, arguing they were overcommitted already with two or even three places. Names were tossed on the table, shuffled with a Governorship already taken and left in abeyance. Finally I found myself with a Governorship. Christ, I was terrified. Such people had always been God to me during my school days, such as they were, back in the 1930s and early 1940s – I had, in the main, been occupied potato planting or picking, sugar beet hoeing and harvesting, haymaking, etc., during the 1939–45 war. I left at fourteen, in 1945 just as the Masters returned from the war, with 'Retarded' on my final report. When I say 'Masters' returning it is an important point – pre-war, women were not allowed to teach once they got married.

Why had filling School Governorship places become such a drag?

There were twenty-nine schools and only fourteen Labour Councillors and (then) most schools needed a whole handful of Councillors on their Boards. Agreed, the Controlling Group would thin down the posts held by Labour Councillors when they went through our list – but it still left everyone with two or three Governorships, because the Tories had the same problems filling their posts.

Allocating School Governorships at that initial Group

Meeting, difficult as that became, paled into insignificance when the Group Leader next called 'Outside Bodies!' for a start I did not know what he meant!

It turned out that no fewer than fifty-one further organisations needed from one to six Councillors on their Committees to represent the District Council's interests – especially where Grant Aid was concerned.

Here and there along the list members did have a genuine interest in the subject, or were keen to be involved in the likes of Citizens Advice Bureau, Council for Voluntary Services, Race Relations Council, a Community Project or the Community Health Council – but even that did not always solve the problem. For example, the Community Health Council is almost a job in itself. It entails very long Agendas, daytime Hospital Inspections, special Sub-committees and Study Groups to provide information for the Government on wide-ranging health subjects including Special Facilities for the Disabled, the need for a New General Hospital or a report on 'Human Fertilisation and Embryology'. Who would have the time or could get time off work to apply themselves to such subjects seriously, even where the inclination existed in the first place?

But there were fifty-one such Outside Bodies – some needing more than one Labour Councillor. Who in the Labour Group was interested enough to spend valuable time on such Committees as 'Warwick Racecourse Limited', or 'Newbold Comyn Golf Club' (both on Council-controlled land), Coventry Airport Consultative Committee, ditto for Birmingham Airport (noise prints overlapping the District), Post Office Advisory Committee (street naming) and so on for fifty-one Bodies.

Names were thrown on to the Group Meeting table and quickly withdrawn as the member concerned expressed his or her opinion of the suggestion and of the member suggesting it too! 'Some of us have a job to do,' or 'I work out of town, remember,' or 'I'm overloaded with Constituency and Party work, Shadow Chairmanship, Schools and...' were the most printable comments.

It is important to realise that most of us were living pretty full lives even before election. In my own case, I was Secretary/Treasurer of the Allotment Association (eight acres), Founder and Secretary of the eleven-strong Allotment Association Council, Party Branch Chairman and Constituency Treasurer, plus Shop Steward and Union Branch Delegate to the Labour GMC (General Management Committee). Most Councillors are elected because they are known to be effective in the posts they hold and are therefore confidently expected to attend to constituents' complaints and problems with the same conscientiousness. To this add the essential Council Meetings of the four Committees, plus Subcommittees which rapidly spring up from each main Committee, now add two (at least) School Governorships – small wonder posts on another fifty-one Bodies began to look a bit worrying. (I was yet to learn that Councillors are regarded as idle and useless!) Added to this, Outside Bodies held meetings here, there and everywhere – whole towns away sometimes, meetings taking half a day or even a whole day. Christ!

I was not prepared for such a burden and unaware that it was required on top of a 7.30 clock-in start at work. Old timers knew only too well the sheer impossibility of it all if you were to do the organisations justice and maintain contact with your Party and electorate at the same time.

Forthcoming selections and elections have to be won also – which can be very time-consuming.

As our Group Meeting ground to stalemate with about half the Outside Bodies yet to be filled the obvious (and only) solution suggested itself. The two old-aged Pensioners (over seventy) in our ranks would 'do' all those remaining. They would turn up at those they could if only for the company and a cup of tea. Those they could not travel to (ever), well, at least we had not let the Party down – we had supplied a name!

From the final list of nominations presented at the Council AGM the following Wednesday it was obvious the other groups had had the same problem, including the forty-one-strong Controlling Group. OAPs predominated on the Outside Bodies. Subsequently one or two of the most outlandish positions became an inter-Group source of merriment even. Mrs Thatcher might send troublesome Cabinet Ministers to Northern Ireland; we 'threatened' to make them Traffic Commissioners – in Birmingham!

The reader may not believe that Committees can be so burdensome. Read the whole book, then pass judgement is my advice.

Somewhat shaken by my first Group Meeting – only a few days after the euphoria of being elected – I decided to proceed carefully. *There may be more to this Councilling business than meets the eye*, I thought. *Jumping up and down making speeches in Council may not be all there is to it.*

I was soon to learn that even that had its pitfalls.

District Council meetings are based on a cycle of meetings. Usually each Committee meets once per cycle, terminating in a Full Council Meeting. Recommendations made in the Committee meetings are ratified or (rarely) otherwise at the Full Council Meeting. Only then has business been passed although it's more than 99.9% sure to pass once it has gone through the Committee stage because Controlling Groups reflect their majority (or more) at all stages. (There are a few exceptions. Plans Committee has delegated authority so that developments, contractors and repairs are not held up. Also Housing Committees may well have two meetings per cycle for the same reason, especially where housing people is concerned.)

The various Committee and Subcommittee meetings

during the cycle are much less formal than the Full Council Meeting where the business is finalised. In ordinary Committee meetings members remain seated when speaking, speak much less forcefully and even speak out of turn or more than once in a debate – depending on the Committee Chairman's leniency.

In many Committee meetings Group tactics may not be pre-decided. An elbow, nudge under the table or a quick word along the line usually suffices to draw a wayward member back to the Party position should one wander when speaking on an important issue. At worst a senior colleague will interject or follow with a correction along the lines of, 'What my colleague is really trying to say…' I found quite a bit of freedom was allowed at this stage especially on Ward issues. However, you spoke strictly to the Party lines in Full Council and woe betide any member putting a foot wrong. It spells trouble with a big 'T' both from his own Group for being out of line with policy or by leaving room for ridicule by members of other groups. In fact if you did not attend the pre-Full Council Group Meeting, the Labour Group did not allow you to speak at all during the Full Council Meeting, unless an exception was granted.

My maiden speech in Full Council left me exposed to the latter – ridicule.

A few evenings before Full Council Meetings all Groups meet (separately) and go through the Council Summons (Agenda). Not only are tactics discussed and policy decided but the main speaker and seconding speaker for main issues are arrived at, spreading the load where possible. Others are prodded to support in varying degrees depending on the principles and/or issues involved. Not only is the order of speakers decided, but it is understood that no member should speak on an issue in Full Council unless given the OK by the Group. The thrust of any speech, supporting or independent, on a local Ward matter is also agreed, of course. This is essential if a small Group is to be effective at any level in politics.

Thus it was that I got the nod to speak on a problem particular to council-house tenants in my Ward – roaming 'packs' of dogs!

No one advised me that roving (randy) dogs was not a good subject to base a maiden speech on. When delivered in a working-class Welsh-border accent in the heart of Royal Leamington Spa it became hilarious, not helped by the fact that I was determined to play it straight the more they howled at me, and I do mean 'howled'.

With a three-to-one majority against me and their Tory nominee in the Chair, I was the one told to shut up and sit down by the Chairman. But I had put a Resolution which gave me the right to reply. A few well-aimed opening caustic remarks when exercising my right to reply ensured I finished that speech off, and a Dog Catcher was eventually appointed to deal with the problem. Young mothers with toddlers and their arms full of shopping (which the dogs are after) can get very frightened when surrounded by ten or twelve dogs each bigger than their little kiddies. The dogs ravage the shopping once it is released if the mothers pick up the kiddies to protect them – but who might get ravaged if she clings to the shopping? Some of the Doberman, Alsatian or Boxer dogs were as big as small donkeys and half starved after roving free all day while their 'owners' were at work. I thought it a serious subject – a two-year-old toddler was like a rag doll to such dogs. This was pre-Parliament interest in the subject, of course.

Ah, well! At least I made my maiden speech in the very first Full Council and went on to become a leading speech-maker for the Group. One colleague never got as far as a maiden speech during his four-year term of office. Another stormed out of the Chamber halfway through his maiden speech and never spoke again. Subsequently, years later, leading Conservative members were to apologise to me, one even saying that he had never felt so ashamed of his Group's behaviour before or since. Be that as it may, in my opinion it was standard practice not only to put you down for the duration of your four years in office but also to ensure you would not stand for office again.

Budding Councillors be warned: pick the subject matter of your maiden speech very carefully, keep it short and stick it out irrespective of the taunting.

Membership of Outside Bodies

As mentioned in a previous chapter, more than eighty Outside Bodies (including the twenty-nine schools) needed District Councillors on their Committees – plus five county-maintained Youth Centres. Six Councillors were needed for some but only one for others. 169 places needed to be filled in all by fifty-eight Councillors (now reduced by the Boundaries Commission to forty-five Councillors). Bear in mind also that each Councillor already had at least four main Council Committees plus two or three Subcommittees depending on how a parent Committee broke down its workload and what issues came to the fore during a Council's lifetime. Also all Councillors were expected to attend the Full Council Meeting plus the preceding Group meeting on top of their Committee commitments.

Chairmen of Committees and, not so frequently, their Deputies and/or Shadow Chairmen need to spend one hour or so before a meeting (or at some time) liaising with Officers on major issues on the Agenda, if only to avoid looking fools in the Committee itself.

Refuse collection strikes, major building developments concerning contractors and/or their architects, rating levy proposals, all required Councillors to spend many more hours – perhaps days – closeted with Chief Officers and/or in Public Forums. Actual Council meetings might be held during the evenings, in the main; however, some day commitment would be essential even for conducting normal Council business and some Subcommittees must meet during the day, for example site meetings or joint staff/Councillor meetings with Shop Stewards.

Outside Bodies could be equally demanding of evening and daytime commitment.

I started quietly with just one School Governorship, the Warwickshire Environmental Protect Council (an all-day meeting) and the Council for Voluntary Services. However, as lesser souls in the Controlling Group dropped by the wayside I was to add another school, Marriage Guidance Council and (most dreaded of all) the Community Health Council – but I dropped the CVS appointment, being displaced when the Liberals claimed it. I like to think I left my mark on them all.

School Governor meetings were the most straightforward, as one would expect in the academic world. However, occasionally I was called to Special meetings to shortlist a Head (twice), consider a parents' petition, or ratify (or otherwise) expulsion of particularly wayward children (three times – involving seven children in all). I was on the Boards of Middle Schools but you wouldn't believe the things eight- to twelve-year-olds get up to. Someone has to sort it all out and the buck stopped with the Governors.

On top of continual classroom defiance, bad (foul) language, threatening and bullying behaviour you must add thieving, stabbing and repeatedly playing truant – walking out any time they thought fit only to hang around the area taunting other pupils either directly or through the classroom windows.

Playing truant, you might think, is a non-school activity, but when picked up by Police in school hours it was assumed by the Police (probably because they knew the uselessness of trying to get a responsible attitude from parents of such children) that the school would take responsibility for them. Often children were too young to be charged with the crimes they were caught committing – and they knew it! Thus a family of three, led by the sister, were returned from Birmingham one day. Having worn their welcome out in the Leamington area, they had caught the train to Brum to practise their particular art of knocking on doors asking for a drink of water. Once inside the home of an old person – who always took pity on them – they pinched the Pension Book and ran to the nearest Post Office, where they explained that the old person was ill and that they had been sent to collect their pension for them.

Police (and often the public) expect schools to cure this type of behaviour. What were they to do with eight-, nine- and ten-year-olds, or for that matter what could Magistrates do with them?

So they were to be dealt with by the schools – and that meant the Governors sooner or later.

Ah! Yes. Special Schools were provided for just such children as are home studies from a visiting teacher where more than one child in a family was involved and when mixing with other children had such disastrous results for one and all, including teachers, who were not specialists with rebellious children. Such Special Schools and methods use trained staff to deal with these cases. Just who would take on such a job I've yet to discover, but apparently there are teachers who do it – between nervous breakdowns. Still, let's transfer them; the Governors all agree.

Cracked it! Back to work, we the Governors, go…

No way! Such straightforward avenues as transferring them to Special Schools are not on, as the Education Officer reminds us. First, all such schools and placings are over-subscribed and have long waiting lists of wayward children from all over the county. Second, transferring them is not allowed. The system is not set up to accommodate such humane solutions. Special Schools for wayward children and home teaching are only available for children with no school to go to, and these children are still at school – on paper. No way could officers think of trying to accommodate them when they are 'at' school. (And they keep such straight faces as they report and repeat this cast-iron ruling.)

The solution? Such children have to be expelled from school first, then all other schools in the area have to refuse to take them. By that point six months or so will have gone by and the children have convinced themselves they have beaten the system, and are making very adequate livings to boot. Then, lo and behold, a nice clean-cut young man in a pinstripe suit turns up and announces he has found a Special School – just turn up next Monday at nine and all will be well!

Some hope! It's like asking Al Capone to go straight voluntarily – and sit still for hours on end in the bargain.

But none of that is my worry. All I have to do – with my fellow Governors – is to expel them, severing the last tenuous connection they have with a regulated day, school meals (which they turned up for) and a socialisation process.

Would you believe it? Mr Nice-Guy who electors thought looked harmless on the Election leaflet is now sitting round a table expelling their kids from school.

Well, it's not quite like that. I like to think the people who are responsible enough to turn up and vote have brought up well-behaved, keen-to-learn-and-enjoy-school-type children. We had such children very much in mind when the last resort of expulsion was applied to the few (very few) totally wayward ones who caused so much disruption in school.

In any event such drastic decisions were not taken without studying reams of reports from numerous teachers (often from more than one school) and from various Welfare Agencies. We then interviewed current teaching staff, Agency staff (or Supervisors) and parents (if they turned up), very carefully, slowly and deliberately. I tried to visit homes as well, but often this proved too difficult.

Parents lived apart; were not in; addresses changed frequently; or they just would not open doors (fearing a debt collector I assumed). Even late in the evenings I failed to make contact – although the children were still out and about the streets, telling me their parents were away in the most unlikely places, for example Scotland.

Did you know that these are the duties you line a Councillor up for when you vote? Did I know when I stood to be a Councillor? No way!

Other School Governor duties were also additional to formal Quarterly Meetings and less arduous, in fact, decidedly pleasant.

Until I had trouble getting a Pass Out from work the Christmas lunchtime cup of tea and a mince pie fell into this category. I would lose about thirty minutes from work only (because school dinner hours are earlier than works) but a friendly 'Thank you' to all the school staff – playground ladies, cooks, helpers, cleaners and lollipop ladies/men as well as to the teachers – seemed to go down very well, I thought. It introduced a new face and a handshake in the same way Senior Supervisors came round the factory floor at Christmastime in those days. However, the same Supervisors were soon to prevent me from returning the compliment to 'my' staff in the schools.

In turn I think the staff genuinely liked to see a Governor and his wife on such occasions. It gave them a feeling of belonging perhaps, being noticed, particularly in the case of the manual staff who are usually unable to get to, or not invited to, the more formal evening events. Also Heads and Deputies (perhaps Teachers) were glad to show a little appreciation – in the form of a cup of school tea and a bun – to someone who had turned up and helped formalise a tricky situation here and there during the year.

Another Outside Body on which I represented Warwick District Council was the Warwickshire Environmental

Protection Council. My involvement on this body was to get me into trouble over microwave ovens but it also gave me the opportunity to inspect factories, food processing, packing and distribution centres, a smokeless fuel processing plant (a filthy place), a nuclear power station (beautifully clean but what unseen dangers?), an oil refinery (where Shell staff took the mickey), numerous gas and electrical centres and depots, a waterworks and reservoir. I discussed farming methods with top National Farmers' Union Officers and kept in constant discussion with senior Environmental Officers of four Districts adjoining one another (Stratford-upon-Avon District did not join in at that time).

This last aspect was the main reason for the Environmental Council. Neighbouring Districts in a county could co-ordinate their efforts, share research, development, equipment, findings and expense and thus avoid duplication but arrive at common standards, interpretations and inspection procedures. Thus Contractors, British Rail, Motorways and Water Authorities, even mobile members of the public would not be faced with differing requirements each time they crossed a District boundary within the county.

Unfortunately, only four of the five Warwickshire Districts co-operated in this way. Stratford-upon-Avon declined, arguing their very rural area did not fit into our pattern (the rotten lot) but Coventry had just joined, at their request, at the time of my departure when my Councillor position ended. It was a Committee I enjoyed. I felt I learnt something in return for a modest input – unlike other Committees, which exhausted you for little return.

The microwave oven incident is dealt with under Studies in the sixth chapter. Members on this Committee, both elected and professional officers, were very supportive – it was that kind of a Committee. Cut and thrust of Party politics did not come into it, nor should they where Environmental Health is concerned, or health of any kind for that matter.

In the same vein I was elected Chairman for the year when Warwick District was host and provided both facilities and committee officers for the year. This was unusual for a minority Group member. However it turned out to be a fruitful year and I was pleased with the warm handshakes and congratulations whoever they came from. The experience did me no harm – microwave ovens and all.

For years I served on the Community Health Council. That was an exhausting Committee, that's for sure. There were daytime Hospital Inspections leading to compiling a report for the full-time paid Committee Secretary to print up. These reports were released to the press and public via the minutes of the next full meeting. All hell broke loose if hospital staff, patients or public disagreed. Such outbursts were frequent because we interpreted our role as being critical observers of establishments, Government plans and even of publications of proposed legislation. (Other CHCs interpret their roles differently. They vary from Government lapdogs to upholders of anti-Government stances which include organising street demonstrations.) However, critical dissection of other people's professions by well-meaning outsiders can stir up vigorous rebuttals.

So be it. At least it keeps everyone informed and staff on their toes.

It was necessary to form Subcommittees to comply with Health Ministry requests for comments on Government reports and proposed legislation, some of which made very far-reaching recommendations and changes to aspects of the Health Service. Thus it was that I came to do a paper on 'Human Fertilisation and Embryology', i.e. test-tube baby developments. Did my electorate really elect me with this in mind? Well, the Government wanted the 'Public's' response and to obtain this in an organised way and by a certain date the appropriate Ministry contacted appropriate committees which had public representatives on them. I was on a watchdog Committee for the Health Service, therefore I was the member of the public to respond on behalf of my constituents – or so I saw it. (But do the public?)

During my period on the Community Health Council, Phase One of the new Warwick District Hospital was completed. As hospital services concentrated in a modern hospital, smaller outlying hospitals came under threat of closure. Thus it was I completed a study on the advantages (as I saw it) of a purpose-built and equipped District General Hospital. I spoke as an invited speaker on the subject to a public meeting in Stratford Town Hall called to protest against the closure of their Monroe Devis Maternity Hospital.

The audience gave me a very bad time, even if it did broaden the meeting's outlook. Speaking to a Town Hall full-to-standing of hostile middle-class public is not something I would recommend Arthur Scargill to do.

Life was much simpler on my allotments!

Was I still representing the electorate in my Leamington Ward when speaking in Stratford-upon-Avon's Town Hall? If my constituents wanted an up-to-date, efficient, well-equipped General Hospital to go to when ill, yes I was. It was delayed two years anyway due to The Cuts. But did they see it this way?

I should have stopped to ponder the point then, because soon after the Stratford meeting my Branch declined to reselect me for the Ward.

Some little way into my seven years as a District Councillor I became the District's representative on the Marriage Guidance Council's Executive Committee – now called Relate. At that time the local MG was desperate for money and this was the main topic of the early meetings I attended (attended to their surprise, because they had not seen a Councillor for yonks). I suggested begging letters to be sent to a wide range of organisations in the area the local MG served, Town/Parish Councils, Unions, Social Clubs as well as the usual Lions, Round Table and Doctors' Surgeries. In any event, I outlined the letter in working-class terms: 'If you want a Marriage Guidance service – cough up.' I offered a six-page list of Union Secretaries and Factory Convenors, Trades Councils, etc. for them to contact.

There was shocked silence among the assembled middle-class members and for three successive meetings no letter – although it was always agreed to send one. My frustration was becoming obvious and the MG debts ever bigger. There was even talk of folding up. I threatened to name names (publicly) where the stagnation rested. Finally they broke their stiff-upper-lip middle-class code and circulated fifty letters to addresses already supplied by me, plus more to their normal contacts, of course.

One Town Council took exception to the 'put-your-money-where-your-mouth-is' approach and its Deputy Mayor called us 'parasites' when discussing our request in his Town Council meeting. A member of the public came back at him from the Public Gallery during the public debate time at the end of the meeting (allowed in Town/Parish Councils – but not in District or County Councils).

The MG immediately hit the headlines and bang went their middle-class image, of course. Consternation. How long would I have lasted if I had not been drafted on to their committee?

However, the resulting counterblast and the Deputy Mayor's published letter of apology all helped to get the Marriage Guidance Service well publicised. Clients and money poured in – from Town Councils, Doctors'

Surgeries, Factory Social Clubs plus satisfied ex-clients and well-wishers whom I had not thought of 'tapping up'. In fact the publicity proved so effective that a £150-per-year advertising bill was saved and existing client contributions (not fees, but voluntary) went up in leaps and bounds also. On top of this I was appointed Press Officer for the local MG – a position I thought of, and filled, tongue-in-cheek, being unfamiliar with their tactics and day-to-day running methods.

Subsequently a move to bigger, warmer, better-laid-out offices next door (with more privacy for clients) was required to cope, and even more money was required for office shelving, equipment, a photocopier, books for increased staff, a filing cabinet and electric typewriter. Thus it was that I came to promote a 'Marriage Guidance Fund Appeal' raffle both to raise money and to get MG on to the shop floor and into homes via the raffle tickets. This raffle became an annual event raising several hundred pounds each year. No doubt it helped me get re-elected onto the MG Executive Committee as a 'loved and cherished' member, even after my duties ceased as a District Council representative.

I assumed some of my electorate had need of its services therefore I considered it my Councillor duty to ensure its survival. Other District Councillors representing the District on other Outside Bodies no doubt gave their support and talents likewise – perhaps that is why the number of Outside Bodies needing a Councillor representative keeps increasing year by year.

On being elected to the District Council an outgoing Councillor handed over the Chairmanship of the Youth Centre within the Ward. I was elected to the position on his recommendation and in my own right – another District Councillor represented the Council's interests. I therefore continued in this post after my period as Councillor ended.

However, a tie-up with the District Council did occur as a result of this position and landed me the Chairmanship of a local football team to boot.

This football team used the Youth Centre to train in and had applied to the District for a grant – along with many, many other teams and sporting organisations who got annual grants in the main.

Being a member of the District Finance Committee I was present and defended the football club when the Officer's recommendation not to make a grant came forward. The club was in a deprived area (second most deprived Ward in the County according to the Townsend criteria); nearly all its players were unemployed, struggling to establish the team against all the odds in a fairly major league – Coventry and District. I spoke accordingly, of course.

A lot of whispering then took place between the District Treasurer and the Finance Committee Chairman. The Chairman asked my connection with the club. More whispering. I thought I must have put my foot in it – this sort of whispering in Committee being most unusual. Not so! The Treasurer announced to the Committee that his greatest difficulty was to find a reliable person with whom to deal on behalf of this football club. They had had seven Club Treasurers in the previous twelve months and he had no confidence that they were capable of reducing their £133 overdraft at the bank. However, if he could pay a grant to the Youth Centre where I, as its Chairman, would ensure it was used correctly as a priming grant for the new football club then he would change his recommendation.

Thus I became Chairman of a football club in my Ward because subsequently it was found unconstitutional for the Youth Centre to cash cheques for an affiliated user of the premises.

Running a football club turned out to involve monthly

Sunday night meetings (largely debating unpaid subs, fines and pitch fees), transporting players all over the County on Sundays and trying to reconcile players to a realisation that they should replace beer with food, and nights on the town with training sessions, and retain a small amount of their Supplementary Benefit for Club dues. It proved an impossible task and two years later, when the overdraft was finally cleared, the club folded. Only the overdraft in the Manager's and Secretary's names kept them battling against all the odds for that long, in my opinion.

Along the way I had forfeited many Sunday afternoons and Sunday evenings, spent about £100 in petrol, sold raffle tickets, collected jumble, recruited players on their behalf, and talked, and talked, and talked trying to get sense into them, none of which stuck. Three were arrested and jailed for murder a few years later.

However, all was not wasted. A younger second team had also played one full season by then and a five-a-side junior team had played friendlies under their colours. This junior team and the team Manager were to turn into a full team for the Youth Centre – a development I had spent years trying to get started, but all formal approaches had proved abortive.

Things sometimes move in mysterious ways.

All this football work was in my Ward, therefore it could fairly be argued to come within the duties of a District Councillor elected by that Ward. However, some questioned that reasoning – certainly my family did. Car, petrol, time all going down the drain was the way they saw it and riding in a car after six or seven muddy-booted footballers had been in it smoking their heads off can give that impression. It certainly left me too hard up to afford beer and cigarettes. Other aspects might be questionable, such as talking a player out of the Police cells on Sunday mornings so that you could make up a team, or repeatedly chauffeuring players who persisted in winding all the windows down and catcalling after anything in skirts every time I drove through town. This was not the image I wished to portray and some may not call it football either.

Being involved with youth work, a long-standing connection one way and another, opened up other avenues of activity for me. When the Central Area Gala Day Committee formed I was elected its Treasurer. This in turn necessitated my wife and I getting very involved in the build-up to, and on the day of, the one-day Gala event which brought together Youth Clubs and Youth Organisations from a wide area. This I continued of course, irrespective of Council positions held or not held.

I was also elected, via the Chairmanship of the Youth Centre, into the Youth and Adult Education Committee and again continued in this office after my fall from grace as a Councillor.

One post I did lose during my term of office as a Councillor was the Secretary/Treasurer post of the allotment site – the site was being built on! However, membership of Outside Bodies on the District Council's behalf had expanded my interests somewhat to replace this activity. Being Secretary/Treasurer of an allotment site and fighting off the Council's Notices to Quit had proved a useful testing ground (allotments, testing ground – a joke). Even when I had lost a lot of Outside Bodies as a non-Councillor I still retained the Chairmanship of a Youth Centre, Treasurership of the Central Area Youth Gala Day, membership of Youth and Adult Education Committee and the post of Press Officer of Marriage Guidance Council. Moreover contacts at work continue and workmates (7,200 employees) still use me for advice concerning where to get forms, drafting letters, whom to contact, as per 'Surgery' inquiries in my Councillor days.

Councillors' 'Surgeries'

Car park Surgeries in the Ward were held every Saturday morning throughout the seven years I was a District Councillor. We took it in turns, but someone was in Crown Way Shopping Precinct car park every Saturday morning between eleven and twelve noon – whatever the weather.

Advertised indoor Surgeries were also held on the last Thursday in the month in the Community Centre – for one hour before Branch meetings.

Not many people attended the advertised indoor Surgeries, except when something unusual occurred, for example Gypsies moved into the Ward or when a street disturbance had kept a whole street awake (usually the last straw in an ongoing noisy neighbour situation). Otherwise it served as a place to regularly meet the Chairman and Secretary of the Tenants' Association who updated me with written lists of repairs needed to lifts, stairways or lights in blocks and streets; problems with refuse collection, grass cutting, overgrown street trees, vandalism; kids on roads, in alleyways… you name it they get there. (And then do things I never dreamed of as a youngster!) With over 3,000 council dwellings (half the Council's stock) in one Ward there were a lot of youngsters about, especially those from five-, eight- and fourteen-storey blocks.

On the other hand the car park Surgeries were always busy for me (perhaps not for others) and I often did not get away until 1 p.m.; sometimes not until 1.30 or 2 p.m. Staying later did not bother me, but I lost two hours overtime at work in order to get there for 11 a.m. The car park Surgeries were unclaimable because only one Surgery per month can be claimed and the £5 for that did not even cover the hire of the room.

There is no money to be made out of Council duties. In fact the loss-making situations got even more frequent as my 'tour of duty' extended and my interests and activities increased, including petrol for transporting footballers about.

Typical complaints at a Car Park Surgery would be overdue repairs to council dwellings, for example crumbling floors from the swelling-up infill used; rain leaking in via flat roofs on porches, balconies or top-floor flats; rotten front or back doors, windows, fencing, guttering; rubbish (old mattresses, etc.) dumped in connecting back alleyways; learner scooter riders using these alleys as race tracks; leaking internal plumbing unattended for months or years after initial reporting of the faults to the Housing Department; and continuous transfer requests from high- and low-rise flats because of damp and mouldy conditions and misuse of stairways, landings or lifts by strangers, intruders or teenagers.

The tenant who holds my record for awaiting repairs was a householder who had been put off for twenty-one years – her council house was parting company with the semi next door! The whole estate had been built over a thirty-metre-thick layer of sand. The crack outside had got a gooseberry bush growing in the rotting birds' nest where the crack widened up near the eaves – a self-set bush grown up from a dropped seed. This crack, of course, manifested itself right through the house – bedroom walls parting from the dividing wall (repeatedly filled with every redecoration), the airing cupboard parted likewise and so to a similar crack right down the rear wall.

This was eventually attended to, but only after the houses had been white coated outside! She now lives with an even bigger strip of new cement running from foundations to eaves – an eyesore and a continual reminder still.

Others had waited fifteen years to get huge earthquake-type upheavals across kitchen floors repaired. A major job, I know, necessitating moving the families out into temporary accommodation for six to eight weeks, but it had to be done; why leave families under such stress for so many years? Kids become wild; parents alcoholics from the stress.

Besides the repair-type complaints, other tenants were desperate to get transferred out of high-rise flats, away from condensation problems causing damp, mould creating a nauseating smell that clung to clothes even when worn. Quite apart from the problems of existing council-house tenants I received complaints and requests for help from people, young and old, needing accommodation, or transfers from expensive private lettings. Some had problems that were the responsibility of other Council Departments, e.g. uncut grass, overgrown trees, lorries churning up grass verges and so forth – Amenities Department; badly maintained roads, pavements, blocked gullies, street litter – Planning Department; dog nuisance, refuse collection – Environmental Health Department. Occasionally an issue needed the Police attention, the Council Solicitor or another agency such as Citizens Advice Bureau, Community Health Council, Electricity Board, Gas Board or Water Authority.

All these matters I noted and took up with the appropriate Department or Agency via a memo – where verbal advice and passing on an address or contact was insufficient.

On being elected to the District Council I received, with the very first mailing, a memo pad. I religiously used these memo pads, retaining a carbon copy of each complaint taken up that needed a written follow-up. Not only did I have a record to refer back to – and read to the constituent the following week or so – but more to the point, the relevant Department soon realised I had a copy when the second memo quoted the date and details of the first.

I have to say that during the seven years I held office I had early and favourable action on just about 99.9% of complaints taken up in this way. But the first six months – nothing. I then informed the Housing Department by memo that I would be forwarding the twenty-one-year- and fifteen-year-long complaints to the Ombudsman as soon as I had sufficient documented proof of lodged complaints. Bingo! I never had cause to make any such suggestions again. Just as well as it turned out, because Government spending dictates and Rate Capping measures would make it impossible to attend to a twenty-eight-year (by then) backlog of repairs.

As time went on my case load built up as word got around that I would get action. The work involved became a major part of my Councillor duties and involved my wife to an even greater extent too – taking telephone calls, typing more and lengthier follow-up letters to agencies and generally holding the fort at home as such work pulled me out into people's homes inspecting faults night after night. Some issues that arrived via constituent complaints also necessitated attending meetings on their behalf to negotiate items through – or to at least try to ensure a favourable result by my very presence.

The carbon copies retained in the memo pads can be added up and broken down, and this I did from time to time to make reports to Branch meetings.

In any one memo book of fifty carbon copies the breakdown came out at about twenty-odd housing complaints for the Housing Department; three or four for the Amenities Department; ditto Environmental Health, Planning, Chief Executive/Solicitor Departments. Miscellaneous agencies such as Police, Water Authority, Electricity Board, Gas Board would add up to about five in total out of the fifty.

The remaining five or six would be repeat memos chasing up a previous one where no action had resulted or where new information had come to hand.

I completed twenty-one memo books in seven years, that is, averaging over 130 separate new complaints per year – but they peaked during 1981. My problems at work getting time off, plus news of abusive telephone calls and late-night or early morning calls were getting into the press by then, and this frightened or deterred constituents during the last two years. The process stopped abruptly when I was not reselected, leaving my last five months almost void of complaint work. Thus in 1981 I wrote 188 memos of which 132 were initial complaints. Added to the memo total must be numerous phone calls, about as many again complaints dealt with verbally with no record but using my experience, of course, plus some much longer typed letters and submissions involving my wife's help for the more persistent causes such as evictions, tribunals and mouldy and damp dwellings. These condensation problems remained with me irrespective of how often the dwellings had a change of tenant; individual tenants' problems may be solved or eased by a transfer, but not mine. The next tenant in was contacting me about six months later.

At the very least all 1,050 memos received one reply from Officers/Agencies, the core of which had to be passed on to the constituent involved, of course.

A more persistent case was that of the Still family, a young mother and husband plus one child. Mrs Still became pregnant again during the 'battle'. Fortunately she just – only just – got rehoused before the second baby arrived. If it had been a boy she was going to name him after me!

Basically the Still family's predicament was no different from that of thousands of others up and down the country and scores more within my Ward. However, the Stills came to me. They were not the first with such a problem, but the first I decided to stand and fight for via press articles and headlines. The young couple were very pleasant and presentable. Sue had a winning cockney accent as well. I was waiting for such a couple with nerves of steel, a young child and who were reasonably turned out. I needed one such case to get into the press so that others could also reap the benefits if we won it. Therefore everything had to go right – to lose it would have the reverse effect. Even the second pregnancy was discussed in advance and timed perfectly for maximum effect in the press. (Only a London couple would have this sort of trust in their Councillor!)

Initially housed by Warwick District as homeless when they arrived from London, they were in temporary accommodation because they had voluntary vacated their Housing Association flat in London. Now their temporary and extended temporary period was up and out into the streets – furniture, belongings and baby, they had to go. This was normal practice countrywide, but here let me say a word in favour of Warwick District's policy of housing 'intentionally' homeless. Warwick District allowed an initial three months. Most Districts/Metropolitan Councils allow only seven days, even Labour-controlled ones.

Reasons such as following her mother into the area to be near her mum at baby time and away from the unsavoury neighbours and area in London, plus job hunting in Leamington's comparatively affluent area for husband Mick – none of these issues mattered. They had made themselves 'intentionally' homeless, while 3,000-odd were 'patiently' waiting on Warwick District's waiting list, so out they would have to go before the risk of a twelve-month continuous tenancy made them permanent tenants in the eyes of the Law.

Their rent was paid up here and elsewhere (eventually). They had been quiet neighbours. They had even redecorated parts of the flat (under my advice). They had no convictions or bad record (although Mick was to get into a fight under the stress of it all and get himself fined) – but still out they must go. Only a week's extension, followed by another week, followed by a freeze pending a Court Appeal instigated by me. The fight was on.

It all made headlines. It broke your heart – touched even the most ardent adherent to the waiting-list model. Even the 'Judge' (Registrar) at the Hearing criticised the Council – but only granted a further temporary stay before enforcing eviction with the full backing of the declared Law now. It's a dangerous road to tread, headline-getting for the greater good, and Mrs Still was well and truly pregnant again by now! Life was less nerve-racking as an allotment organiser, I can assure you.

All's well that ends well. They obtained a Housing Association's tenancy just in time, with only days to spare. I had kept young Mick Still walking around the twelve Housing Association offices throughout the battle. Just as well.

Would I have taken time off work to barricade their flat against the Bailiffs as I promised the Stills I would? I just do not know, but that was the plan.

I point out this story so that readers can judge that even two to four new complaints per week do not tell the half of it sometimes. I calculated that a Councillor, with his own full-time job, could not carry emotionally more than two persistent cases at any one time on top of all the other duties involved in being a Councillor. Memos to the relevant Department/Agency are the least part of it in some cases. Telephone calls (and expense), drafting letters, wife's typing, house calls explaining step-by-step action to clients and drafting Court/Tribunal submissions for them can be very time consuming. But nerves of steel and an ability to keep one step ahead are also needed.

A much less happy ending to a transfer request was the case of a mother and two daughters of approximately twenty years old. They were trapped in a five-storey block of flats, the mum having put in for a transfer to a house and garden as soon as the first daughter had arrived some twenty-one years earlier. When the second daughter arrived the pressure had built up and the father had departed. I took up their case on the basis of length of time on the waiting list (larger families continually jumped over them on the list – they went downwards on the list and not upwards and out); unsavoury goings on in the whole block; equally unsavoury character of the communal landings and hallway (how were the girls to get back home from a night out with no dad to escort them to and fro); the ongoing health effects of the black mould in all such flats not to mention the resulting smell on their best evening dresses. After a few memos to the Housing Department pressing their case, I arrived one Saturday lunchtime hot foot with a copy of a letter granting their transfer request to a Council House only to find suited, sombre men lining the stairway all the way up to their second-floor flat. The family had received a similar letter in the post the morning before and mum and daughters had spent that day excitedly shopping for small decorative items for the 'new' house. Clang! Mum had passed away in her sleep during the night. What could I say to her distressed daughters? Fortunately a flat full of women relatives had arrived up from South Wales, hence the suited, sombre menfolk lining the stairway.

It knocked me for six and some more. Some knocks are harder to take than others.

An ever-increasing part of my duties was to draft letters for constituents. On a few occasions I even filled in forms for constituents and was called out by a phone call on one occasion to do just that. Advice on where to get appropriate forms was always in demand – Town Hall, Job Centre,

Citizens Advice Centre, Community Project, Claimants Union, Post Office. Some you kept to hand.

Where to obtain the form was not the real question behind many approaches; they could have walked into the Post Office behind me in the car park and found that out or even collected the right form while in there. Whoever mans Councillor Surgeries has to be able to give a fairly accurate idea whether the inquirer is likely to succeed with their claim. Thus it is information on Sup-Ben, Fuel Allowances, Travel Claims, Free School meals and so on that they are really after, plus someone to build their confidence up to a point where they feel at ease making their claim as the right of a citizen and not as an handout to a beggar.

None of this counselling will appear on Councillors' memos anywhere, nor is it recognised by the public or even by Party members and certainly not by a spouse left deserted at home.

And yet I would suggest two and a half new cases per week at the peak, an average of two per week over a seven-year period is a fairly large memo case load before you add verbal advice, counselling, drafting letters, house calls and attending tribunals.

But there were holiday periods? Holiday periods – you say!

It's true I had my annual two-week holiday with my family each year. I always took the view that my family deserved to see that much of me. Besides, I was the only driver, so they would not get far without me. Also Council and Agency Offices are closed at weekends and on bank holidays – staff everywhere get those times off.

Not so a Councillor. I have been called out on Christmas Eve and Boxing Day. Bank holidays and weekends were the worst for telephone calls – especially between midnight and 1.30 a.m. on Saturday nights. Such calls went in spates and were genuine in the main, for example a disturbance where noisy neighbours were keeping 'half the neighbours' awake. If a constituent had already reported such a problem via a Surgery I would always advise a course of action including, 'Keep me up to date or I will assume the problem has been solved.' When better to update me than when it is actually happening? After all there is not much else you can do at that time of night once your television viewing or sleep has been disrupted and the noise continues.

Such phone calls disturbed my whole family, of course. My wife was not amused – especially when it took a further thirty minutes or more to calm the caller down and my voice echoed throughout the whole house at that time of night. My children had mock O levels, O levels and A levels – just like any other teenagers. A disturbed night, or nights, did not help one little bit – as my constituents experienced, hence their complaints about their noisy neighbours.

I was called out by phone at four o'clock one morning. I settled the old lady's nerves by chatting to her for an hour or so while the Police, who I had called before leaving home, explained the difficulties to a new eighteen-year-old single-parent tenant still decorating in the flat above. High-heeled shoes on bare floor boards plus continually dropping the scraper as weak hands gave out is not an ideal background noise for a seventy-nine-year-old to sleep to. They take a tablet, wake up and take another, wake up and can't remember if they had only one tablet or not and take another one anyway. The next time they are awakened they think it's morning, get up only to find it's not. Confused, they take another tablet and it's anybody's guess if they wake up again – ever.

I always advised old people on their own to ring me before they started on the sleeping tablet roundabout.

'Only a phone call away' our Councillor's card said and every year the Branch distributed cards to every house in the Ward saying just that.

Anyway, it was the least I could do for them in my opinion. They and/or their menfolk had fought two wars and worked a lifetime for their country. Young people grossly abuse the freedoms the older ones fought and worked to protect, in my opinion.

The difficulty was that word spread. I got even more involved at the expense of my family and home life and, eventually, work commitments too.

Such is the life of a busy District Councillor who runs Surgeries. You finish up at the beck and call of the whole town.

An example of non-recorded advice by a non-constituent of mine is the following case, which I can tell now because he has become a friend, like many other inquirers, and he has the gas bills and letters to hand to recall the step-by-step action.

He first approached me for advice on how to challenge an estimated gas bill which he thought excessive and the chances of success. His mother had had a new gas meter fitted but it had not worked for seven months. This had been repeatedly reported to the Gas Board Office but it still took seven months to get it repaired. Using my usual 'worker' channels I soon discovered why. The local Gas Board Manager had a technique of leaving jobs paid for under the Standing Charge on his desk; he gave out jobs to his workmen which brought in actual money. However, the subsequent official reason for the non-repair was 'don't know'. Meanwhile the estimated bill for seven months was £186 for two gas fires and a gas cooker used by a middle-aged mum and dad – this is around 1980 remember.

On my advice the married son (my inquirer) wrote and asked for an explanation because it was three times higher than any previous bill. We expected to get backlists of bills and previous amounts used.

The Gas Board replied in one sentence: 'It was winter.'

On my advice the son again wrote pointing out that we do not have seven months of winter – what was the average payment over past seven-month periods for similar times of year?

This time the reply was in the form of a very official letter threatening to cut off gas supply if the estimated amount was not paid and that Court action would be taken within seven days, etc., etc., frightening his mum and dad to near death – and making my name mud in their sight at that period, I might add.

Undeterred, he returned to me for further advice – a point of principle coming into it now that threats had been used, exactly the opposite reaction the Gas Board was trying for. But how many people have a Councillor waiting in a car park to strengthen their resolve?

This time I gave him the Gas Consumers Council's address and drafted a letter to them outlining the case so far – for him to write out and send to them – copy to the Gas Board, of course, and retaining one for future reference if needed.

After a delay, the Gas Consumers Council wrote back to the effect that the Gas Board had investigated the case on their behalf (very condescending) but they at least included some figures this time.

1. Consumption for previous winter period – November to February.
2. This November to February bill broken down into daily units used.
3. Period when meter not working 207 days (seven months).
4. 207 × winter daily units – estimated bill of £186.

The Gas Consumers Council was prepared to accept their reasoning and therefore thought there was no case to follow up.

Whether it's old school tie connections or social circles or just 'incompetence – easy way out' I don't know, but that is the usual brush-off from such Agencies for starters.

It put the pressure on me, of course, to apply my brain-power to figures and spend time on them.

Looking back at a stack of old Gas Bills my inquirer had by now armed himself with, it was easy to see the November to February units used were much, much greater than units used in any other months, e.g. 414 compared to 120 for two consecutive bills. The Gas Board did subsequently acknowledge this when pointed out by the inquirer via the Consumers Council and they dropped their estimated bill to £169 – still way above anything paid previously for a seven-month period but it served to rejuvenate my inquirer (and his mum).

My inquirer then pointed out that during the earlier period of November to February on which the estimate was based two sons (one himself) had been at home who had since married and left by the time of the non-working new meter period. When at home they sat up all hours watching television with the gas fire on, eating their mum out of house and home via the gas cooker. Thus on his own account now he still argued £169 was much too high and thought £120 was a more realistic figure. On my advice he offered £120.

The Gas Consumers Council pressed this point and their representative called at the house to say it had been agreed at £136 and advised payment.

The £136 was paid because my inquirer decided it was time to relieve his mother of the constant stress, not because he thought it was a fair estimate even then.

However, despite the payment of £136 a new bill came

from the Gas Board for £159 – less £136. On inquiring at the Gas Consumers Council he is told that while the representative dealing with the case got a verbal agreement for £136, the Chairman of the Consumers Council had gone back on it and agreed to let the Gas Board bill their client for £159.

Needless to say I was right back into the battle – with still no printed material to prove my involvement and 'verbals' between my inquirer and the Gas Consumers Council now getting heated.

There followed another round of drafting letters quoting units used, sons not at home, agreements made when facts were accepted and finally the Gas Board submitted yet another estimated bill of £146 less £136 already paid.

On his own account my inquirer offered to pay the difference if the Gas Board would refund it should the next November to February Bill be considerably lower – this period having already passed, of course, by now.

This offer was refused by the Gas Board on the grounds that 'Customer would have had a chance to prove his point' (presumably he was capable of putting the calendar back).

Hard on the heels of this reply came a letter threatening to cut off the gas again and take the mum to Court for the balance of £10 – despite discussions still going on via the Consumers Council. Seven days or else, were the terms again.

My inquirer wanted to go to Court for a 'fair hearing', especially as the problem occurred because the Gas Board did not choose to repair the meter for seven months. However, the Gas Board had now sent another estimated bill for the following November–February period, making no effort to call and read the meter. The estimate this time was for – three units! Three units as against 414 previously estimated for a similar period. It could only have been so low in order to kill any chance of comparing and, of course, the actual amount used would still have to be paid for when the meter was read eventually, therefore the Gas Board would lose nothing by this ruse.

Of course the Gas Board would not take anyone to Court for £10 – but they would cut off their gas. Thus the onus was on my inquirer to take the Gas Board to Court – while his mum struggled without any gas.

Tied up at work I had never been able to explore Court Injunctions, chances of success, who pays for what, or even how much the costs were – for sure they would be more than £10 even if won – half a day's lost pay at Court would come to that. Thus, unable to advise on how to instigate proceedings for a fair hearing at Court, or estimate the expense, timespan and chances of success, I had to advise my inquirer to pay the £10 however much it went against his feelings.

None of this appears in a Councillor's memo pad or in his re-election address even, nor will Branch or Party members give him any credit for it, still less the general public. Indeed, even the inquirer will eventually drop me out of the story as he tells his mates how he got the bill down by £40. I only ever stood to get the blame if it backfired.

Standing in a cold, wet car park during Councillors' Surgery can be a double-edged weapon. It's a lot warmer and safer working overtime on Saturday mornings, that is for sure.

Dealing with the Press

Any Councillors at District or County level who wish to be elected for a second term of office are advised to get their names in front of the public via the press. For one thing it is a much cheaper way than printing Ward newsletters and there are no distribution worries either; second there is a chance of being actually read whereas political leaflets may well be binned. In any event, once you are established as a fairly prominent member of a Party that Party will expect you to get yourself, the Party and its policies into the press as much as possible. Of course, if you put a foot wrong the same Party members will readily criticise and complain that only Chairmen and/or designated Party spokespersons should speak to the press. This must be borne in mind by any Councillor soliciting coverage. It's a tricky path to follow and many elected members, therefore, fight shy of going to the press at all.

I must admit I pondered this dilemma considerably before plucking up courage and deciding my constituents deserved to know my thinking on issues – not all of them directly Council business anyway. I decided it would be on my head to hold the Ward next time and that would be difficult if voters did not hear from me between election leaflets. The most common doorstep complaint during my first election campaign was, 'We do not see you except at election times.' Why one person with a job, home and family to maintain must find the time to knock on their door regularly when they excuse themselves the effort I have yet to figure out.

True, our weekly car park Surgeries and monthly indoor

advertised Surgeries were designed to offset this dig, but they would only pick up complaints, not get our thinking across. Anyway, more and more constituents might use the Surgeries if the ice were broken by their reading about their Councillor regularly in the press.

Thus it was I wrote to the press a letter expressing the opinion that young unemployed tenants in unsatisfactory high-rise flats with no gardens for their children might be well advised to seek employment and houses in the nearest New Town. New Towns at that time (1976) were encouraging people to move into them, had houses (whole streets of them) standing empty, had link-ups with their local employers guaranteeing a house with a job – they even employed Managers to 'sell' New Towns to one and all. They needed the young families, the young families needed the houses.

I checked this out with New Town Publicity Officers first, of course, and received boxes of handout leaflets by return of post proclaiming all these virtues, plus literature on assisted travel to interviews, home-moving expenses claimable, types of house waiting and on estates with bus services, community centres, schools, parks. It all sounded lovely, but did my constituents know about it?

Two things happened which amazed me at the time and made me wonder if writing letters to the press was something I could handle.

Number one: I opened the paper to find my letter was published under Headlines 'Unemployed Urged to Quit Area' and ' "Go East Young Man" says Labour Councillor', in another paper. A prominent news story not a letter at all. The stories listed points made in my letter as if spoken words, for example '2,577 unemployed', '2,400 families on the housing waiting list', 'many housed wanting transfers to houses' – I sounded very well informed and able to express myself very coherently, which was most unlike me at the time.

The second thing: not a single inquiry came forward, still less a volunteer family to move on or off the waiting list.

However, I received no adverse comments and no compliments either for that matter. Even-stevens you might say – but at least I had not been jumped on by Party guardians for going to the press on my own account. From this thought I took courage.

Before I go on to outline my 'career' as a headline grabber I would like to point out that I now know I was asking the ridiculous of young families. A house and a garden is tempting but unless you offer a trade or profession which is in short supply in the area you wish to move to, no travel or moving assistance is forthcoming. In 1976 the unemployed were almost exclusively unskilled, non-professional people. These same young families with toddlers and more babies arriving needed to be near Mum and relatives at that stage of their lives also. Even a thirty-mile cross-country move for a carless family and with no direct rail links or bus services, might as well be to Land's End.

You learn these things as you get more and more involved with your constituents' problems.

Being green I was not to know either that my letter had been sent to the press during their 'silly season' – July and August. With no meetings and few other activities to report during the summer holiday period they will make headlines out of anything. I was soon to turn this discovery to my advantage, holding items back to release during July and August.

Some examples:

'War clouds as Roughnecks Take Over' – a letter that made a lead story about vandalism in the Ward.

'Tenants Revolt is Boiling Over' – on another summer.

The Still family pending eviction lasted right through

another. Marriage Guidance item for another (held back six months for the purpose) and 'Double Duty not Double Pay' was similarly timed.

In between the silly season letters – most still treated as news items – I kept up letters at about two-monthly intervals. Of course, my speeches and comments in Council got me into the press regularly anyway by then. (And people thought I was a six-foot, broad-shouldered ogre as a result – I'm only five-foot two.)

Few, if any, of my letters to the press actually set out Party Policy point by point – the Constituency Chairman wrote regularly and at some length doing exactly that as one of his functions. (Did anyone ever read such heavy and long letters?) I always angled my letters to the shop floor using short sentences which they could digest and in a chatty vein with Labour policy woven in as applied rather than as set out. Party Policy Statements were much too dry reading for a factory-floor readership. Party handout leaflets used to get up their nose. Buying a Labour Party Raffle ticket was a struggle even and as much political involvement as they could stand. Thus I angled my letters to 'my' factory-floor readership hoping for a drip, drip effect.

I say boldly 'my' readership because not only did I receive regular encouraging comments from workmates but my wife did also from her regular mates on the bus to work and from fellow hospital staff. For example, 'I read all your husbands articles' (everyone refers to any press item as articles), or, 'Where's he gone, I haven't seen him in the press for a few weeks?'

One letter that won me a lot of friends and comment on the factory floor was an indirect dig at institutionalised racism – the unconscious racism that hurts deeply though the perpetrator is totally unaware of the hurt he is causing or that the actions are racist even.

As a supposed Welshman, with a Welsh-border accent, I

had suffered too. When I was a lad of just eighteen, blond hair, skinny and knocking on doors to find digs when first in town in 1949, it came hard to have doors slammed in my face with the comment, 'We don't want Welsh scum here,' spat at you. It was news to me that I was a Welshman! I was born in Herefordshire, albeit only one and a half miles from the Monmouthshire border, and it had never occurred to me that a connection existed or that my border accent was 'funny'. It was news to me too that in 1949, just after a war caused partly by the Master-Race theory of a madman, such racial hatred existed. As far as I knew no one had referred to Welsh servicemen as 'scum' – nor servicemen from Scotland, Ireland, India, Africa, or the West Indian troops either. Yet just four years after they returned to civvy street I found that non-English (in the beholder's eyes) were 'scum'. I was eighteen looking for work and wanting somewhere to sleep – and that made me 'scum'. Anyway, they had advertised for lodgers. I had only called in answer to their advert. It came very hard, very hard indeed. To me, *they* had the 'funny' accents; certainly they had funny attitudes. Their adverts for lodgers would state 'No Irish' or 'Irish need not apply' – what response did Irish get at the doorstep from these 'non-racist' householders?

Of course, within the same year I was a National Serviceman myself serving King and Country – and in a Warwickshire Battalion at that. No one said they did not want me then, but comments like 'Welsh Mountain Goat' and 'Sheep Shagger' became the norm, both in and out of the Army; therefore, thirty years on it's easy to spot institutionalised racism whether it's intended or otherwise.

With this in mind I wrote a letter to the press criticising a previous contributor who had complained bitterly about a hole in the road outside his house which had an 'Irishman sitting in it' – Mr McCavity, no doubt! I also criticised the Editor for not editing such a 'slip of the pen' out. I pointed out that buildings, roads and bridges were built by Irishmen the Western world over, but the planners got the honour and credit. A hole that annoys is automatically the fault of an Irishman who was 'observed from my window' by the writer. Planners were now excused from responsibility for an unwanted hole in the road.

Scratch anybody in Leamington and you find an immigrant underneath, because the town boomed from a village of just 300 people to a town of 45,000 in the past 150 years or so. Obviously many, many recent immigrants were from Ireland – the majority of recent immigrants I would judge – many transferring from Cork Ford's works to Ford's Leamington Foundry in the first place and hence into other jobs leaving vacancies for more transfers within Ford's internal structure. Families and relatives followed once a base had been established locally and complete extended Irish families are commonplace to this day – their children and grandchildren are English, of course, but have to take the racial knocks.

My 'Irish' letter expressed a point they had longed to express – as indeed I had for the previous thirty years. When the original letter of complaint was again published in the weekly version of the same paper the 'Irishman sitting in the hole' was left out. At least the Editor got the point and I had got a bit of Socialist equality over to the public hopefully – either way it made me very popular with the Irish in both Irish Clubs in town.

Not all my letters were so subtle, of course, and when the Tory Government started introducing Rate-Capping theories, I produced some serious (and long) essays to argue for Socialism and Democracy. The time for pussyfooting had passed.

Most people think you are paid by the press, but that is not so in a small town anyway. I never ever received one penny for items supplied to the press, not even the front-page stories and only about half the items were printed anyway irrespective of how much time I had put into them. The more serious ones never made it – which annoyed me – and vital sentences and concluding paragraphs were frequently edited out – which annoyed me even more. At one stage I took to adding a note at the bottom of letters, 'Print as written or do not print at all.'

On the other hand, off-the-cuff throwaway comments in Council could come out as headlines, which is one penalty you must pay once you become newsworthy. Thus 'Councillor's Wife Abused by Phone' – a small point I threw into a debate on the value of the Councillor's attendance money – hit the headlines and killed all phone calls for about two months.

Even more annoying was the non-press coverage of carefully researched and given speeches in Council on major issues. They would be reduced to one or two sentences. Readers did at least know you spoke but probably thought you were stupid if that was all you had to say on important issues. In my opinion this aspect of press coverage is a main reason why Councillors have such a bad image with the public. Such meagre coverage in the press gives no impression that their Councillors have spent their weekend studying lengthy Officer Reports, discussed the issues with colleagues, instigated discussions at Branch and/or Constituency meetings, perhaps even made site visits or looked up references in the library (completely forfeiting family and social life) and then prepared and given at least a ten-minute speech with full back-up material to hand if required later in the debate.

Some of the best speeches never even got a mention – the reporters had gone home hours earlier. Eight o'clockish is their bedtime. Nobody criticises them but Councillors are expected to see the business through on the public's behalf only to be labelled 'idle' for their trouble. 'We never see you except at election times,' is the misleading result of such selective reporting.

And yet most Councillors soon learn that a 'pet' topic will get press coverage and play on it for that reason. Mould and dampness in flats were always good for a story anytime it got mentioned in or out of Council. Tenants could hit the headlines with it without my help, of course, and frequently did.

Attacking inadequate bus services serving my Ward was also popular with reporters whenever mentioned.

Gypsies in the Ward would make three or four weeks of headlines – the press would ring up for comments even.

These latter news items far outweighed the background work needed, yet they made one or more columns where carefully prepared speeches were reduced to one sentence.

From time to time I sent letters to national papers but received no luck, probably because my working-class style did not suit the *Times*, *Observer* or *Guardian* to which I wrote. However, the *District Councillor Review* magazine did publish me several times, notably two letters on mobile-home sites.

My home is only two miles along the road from the Royal Agricultural Show Ground at Stoneleigh in Warwickshire. This show has established itself on this permanent site and for two months or so before the three-day event and for weeks afterwards Contractors and Display staff flood into the area. Landladies and hotels know the ropes and prices spiral accordingly, especially as the influx of foreign reps and buyers increases year by year. It is both convenient and cheaper, therefore, for firms to house their staff in caravans near the Show Ground.

It so happened that several prominent local rugby football clubs already had very well appointed and maintained playing fields in the immediate area and even more adjacent to my home.

These clubs and others cashed in on the need for temporary caravan sites by applying for, and getting, permission to site hundreds of caravans over a short period in the summer.

So far, so good for all concerned.

However, rugby playing fields have to be carefully groomed during the summer growing season, especially so during the few months when no games are played, i.e. right bang on the Show period before and after the first week in July.

Fertilisers are one thing, but weed sprays are highly inflammable. If you spray the pitches, the spaces in between them and around them will be sprayed too – and those were the areas pegged for caravans. Anyway most workmen in the caravans would take short cuts across the pitches to the toilets, showers, bar and lounge facilities. A dry spell was always hoped for over the Show period (but never occurred); a dropped match and hey presto, 200 caravans and their sleeping occupants would get roasted in seconds. On the other hand poison walked into caravans via boots and clothing (as workmen basked in the sun when off duty) could have disastrous results on a reduced scale. Visiting gas-cylinder-supplying lorries could blow up – it happened in Spain.

Such an occurrence would rapidly divert the national press hounds from the Show Ground; they would soon check via the Town Hall that a member of the Environmental Health Committee – past Chair no less of the Warwickshire one – was living less than a mile away, on the same road even. The fact that I was scratching a living all day on the factory floor would be conveniently left out of the résumé, pointing the finger at my incompetence in the affair.

Thus it was that I made it my business via memos to Officers, questions in Council, to see that all necessary facilities, fire points, hoses and regular site visits by Inspectors were enforced. In doing so I learnt a lot about caravan sites – as these were – but also the difference between caravan sites and mobile-home sites and their problems. Hence my letters on mobile homes to the *District Councillors Review* magazine.

Like the second-hand microwave oven problems, the District General Hospital project, the paper on Human Fertilisation and Embryology, my involvement with caravan-site issues had become a serious study in its own right. Indeed such studies had become a part of my Councillor duties from early on and deserve a chapter to do them credit, since it was a study on coal that propelled me into the real limelight locally.

Studies

They started with coal, an unlikely topic in Royal Leamington Spa, or even in Warwick District. However, an Officer's report to the District Council detailed developments to date, and projections for five years, for sand and gravel extraction which was a prominent feature in the District. One sentence in the middle of Conclusions, after assuring us they were keeping everything under review, terminated with the phrase '…and the Warwickshire thick coal seam'.

No such coal seam, thick, thin or variable, had been reported in Warwick District, nor had there been any speculation to my knowledge. Very odd, I thought, that our Officers would be keeping an eye on one – and they already knew it was thick?

The document was passed without comment, merely 'Noted'.

Within the previous twelve months the local Coroner had recorded an Accidental Death of a twenty-three-year-old mining technician who had fallen to his death from a Coal Board drilling rig working in the District 'as part of a countrywide mineral mapping of the earth's crust' according to the Coroner officiating at his Inquest.

No further comments had been made either in or out of the press, so far as I knew, on that twist either.

As I left the meeting referred to above I asked one or two colleagues who were also County Councillors if any Planning Applications for exploratory drilling for this unknown (but thick) coal seam had been received. None had – nor did they attach any importance to the words 'and the Warwickshire thick coal seam'. Just a catch-all Officer's ploy they thought.

And yet why 'thick' if a catch-all phrase? And how come the Coal Board let its rigs out for National Surveys just after the National Plan for Coal booklet had come to the conclusion the country was going to be 42 million tons of coal short per annum by 1985 – seven years hence? The plan hinted that if mines were not sunk pronto and brought into production things would get progressively worse up to the year 2000, the limit of their projections. There was no mention of increased imports to fill the shortfall in 1985 or thereafter.

I pondered this thought as I walked up the street towards my car.

Right next to my car a Senior Reporter or Editor was fumbling with his keys about to get into his car on a cold, wet, winter's night when home was the place to be.

'Have you done any investigative journalism into the mysterious Warwickshire thick coal seam?' I asked him as I slowed up to find my keys sunk deep at the bottom of my overcoat pocket. (Oh the joys of being a Councillor!)

'Never heard of it,' he replied, 'but keep me informed if you find anything out.' He looked keenly up at me, by now guessing I was not passing idle comment.

Nothing more was said and we drove our separate ways home, both now feeling, this needs following up.

Just after the 1914–18 World War my grandfather had committed suicide aged forty-one (leaving a widow and seven children) when he had failed to strike coal in a mining exploit on his Welsh-border farm in Herefordshire.

He had borrowed and mortgaged, mortgaged and borrowed and finally floated five shilling shares, which had been readily snapped up by neighbouring farmers and relatives (he was one of thirteen brothers). Besides, the drilling specialists imported from South Wales were ever-confident. They constantly found black everything except coal. They were near, oh so near, they assured him, right up to the day he committed suicide. Then they packed up and left within the week; their food ticket had gone.

Thus a coal legend was in my blood. I had read anything and everything (precious little) about coal and had listened to and devoured every titbit including the minute handbook by the NCB called 'Plan for Coal'. This little handbook with its introduction by Sir Derek Ezra, then the NCB Chairman, solved the missing 42 million ton problem thus:

- 9 million tons from life extension of pits.
- 13 million tons from major improvement schemes.
- 20 million tons from new mines – 'possibly with greater exploration'.

The new Selby mine(s) had advanced – not gone on tap, but past 'Greater exploration' stage.

Belvoir was explored also and would not produce anything like the quantity now needed – only a modest 2 million tons per annum to add to Selby's target of 10 million. Further, Belvoir had to get through the protracted Public Inquiry stage, which had taken seven years to complete at Selby.

Where, oh where had Sir Derek got in mind for greater exploration that would unearth the 20 million tons from new mines – double the output of super-modern Selby? It had got to be a 'thick' seam. 'Thick', you said it – Warwickshire.

Coal Board rigs in Warwick District mapping the earth's mineral crust when he needed to find 20 million tons of coal in Britain? A likely story!

I thereupon got all the literature, library books and back-dated Selby weekly newspapers and read. I went out and about talking Warwickshire thick coal seam with an air of (apparent) confidence, spicing it up with Selby details as if it were an established fact in Warwickshire. News soon came back via workmates and Councillor colleagues, now with interest awakened. A landlady produced a 'core' of Cubbington coal, from a drill in my very own village. Her two mining engineer lodgers had mounted it on the mantelpiece in their bedsit – much to her disgust.

'Spies' (workmates) using the same local as these (and other) drillers and mining engineers soon filled me in on the details. They boasted of tracing coal right across the District and over the border into Stratford-upon-Avon District. (Shakespeare would be able to come home to a respectable job down the pit even!) Off-duty drillers' chit-chat indicated this was part of a seam stretching from the Nottingham coalfields, via the North Warwickshire pits, under us and perhaps on to the South Coast even. It feathered and faulted and was very deep – too deep to mine with current methods in most places, but they could get it out by using high-pressure remote-controlled water jets. They were drilling exploratory holes to check all this out and they already knew that thick (twenty-foot thick) mineable coal existed north of Leamington Spa, stretching from Coventry, via Kenilworth and curving to Southam. Mineable seams, thicker than anything currently mined in the UK and deposits larger than anywhere in Europe. No wonder Sir Derek was not thinking of importing.

I set out and compiled a six-page report predicting the size, spread and nature of a five-pithead colliery around Kenilworth area within the Warwick District area. It was based on hearsay, forecasts from 'The Plan for Coal', projections to the year 2000 from another miniscule handbook by the Department of Energy called 'Coal for the Future', and using my knowledge of the Generating Electricity Board's requirements (and distribution problems) obtained from Open University studies, plus vivid interpretations, deductions and prophecies of my own, based on the new Selby coalfield development.

My wife had barely finished typing it when a knock came on the front door. There stood the Reporter or Editor I had left looking keenly up at me that evening only some five or six weeks earlier.

'We are short of a lead story for Friday. Did you follow up the coal question?' he inquired without any preamble.

His weekly local paper came out on Friday mornings. By Friday night I was recognised everywhere I went. It is true people joked about the front-page coal story, complete with photograph of me, but they did not ridicule me – it went into so much detail, all told by me.

I was to learn much later the reason for his last-minute search for a good lead story that week. The Chairman of the Council told me the story himself. He (the Council Chairman) was visiting the printing works by prearrangement in his official capacity showing round visiting dignitaries from three twin towns – Mayors, Burgomasters, etc., and their wives. The highlight of the evening was for them to stand on the printing-works floor and watch the greatly blown-up first copy go up on the screen as it was run off the press.

News in the actual making, unseen by human eyes before! Royal Leamington Spa depicted at its best – or so he hoped and fully expected.

Not a word of information had they received of the lead story by prearrangement to add to the occasion.

Clang!

Not only did huge headlines proclaim Royal Leamington Spa was to become a mining town (Arthur Scargill and all!) but it was my opposition-Party much-larger-than-life image that boomed down on them fixing them with a 'Big Brother is watching you' stare.

Years later he confessed to me that he had for once in his life been taken aback and could not find anything to say. Apparently he just stood, gold chain and all, and stared totally engrossed in the story as it unfolded line by line in front of him: plus – the hair – the eyes – the nose – Christ! It's Hughie Griffiths!

The six-page report is yet to be contradicted by anyone; in fact, the Coal Board put me on their mailing list. I got regular quarterly publications from them for several years thereafter.

The County Council (after a circumspect six-month delay) announced that coal had been discovered in the District, and they started releasing bits of information which only confirm my story, but according to them the exploratory drilling only started then and continued thereafter, thus they were not in a position to inform the public earlier – according to them!

I did not believe the Officers at County or District level were unaware of the drilling implications – how could they have been, and yet be able to describe the seam as 'thick'?

At intervals and as topic and time permitted I did similar studies on other issues, some already touched on in earlier chapters.

Renewable sources of energy – solar, wind, wave, geo-thermal and tidal – are a continuing interest of mine. The tidal Severn Barrage study did get a write-up in the local press (in a small way). It is now topical but at the time (1981) a bit before its time and I failed to get a resolution through the Branch (even) for forwarding to Labour Party Conference – the purpose of the study. That same year two resolutions on the subject did appear but they were composited into a Resolution dealing with energy generally (Composite 22 page 245 – Conference Resolutions). It was carried but the Severn Barrage project was reduced to one line in a four-line sentence in the build-up to the main points of the Resolution.

I did manage to get a one-sentence reference to building houses to new 'solar' designs squeezed into Labour's District Manifesto but again no one really wanted to know about such things. They complained bitterly about turning the Manifesto Committee into a Technical Committee.

A study on the advantages of power stations providing piped District Heating (hot water) and electricity convinced me of the need to change the Constitution of the Generating Board. They need to be empowered and compelled to build new power stations, and modify existing ones, to a design that will provide water hot enough to pipe countrywide in a grid system. It would provide cheaper heating in homes, offices, public buildings and hospitals, thus allowing people's budgets to be reallocated to other items such as more suitable diets. Their health could be improved two ways – 'better heating and better eating' (A catchphrase to suit the development). Instigating and installing this system would put money in the pockets of the unemployed, also helping their family's budgets even more directly.

My AUEW Branch usually took more interest than the Labour Party in these issues – and I did get a Resolution on Combined Heating and Electricity through the Branch – only to see it lose at General Management level. It finally got through in 1985, by which time it was Labour Party policy anyway.

Such issues do not have the 'sex appeal' to Party members as do resolutions against The Cuts; reducing housing waiting lists; holding down rents; or about rating problems. It is very difficult to hold the attention of a Manifesto Committee with energy-saving house designs. It is even more difficult to speak to Branches in the heart of England on the need for a Severn Barrage which would produce safe electricity infinitum without nuclear radiation or nuclear waste problems – but with heightened water levels downstream yet to be resolved.

I have never understood why the lack of interest. Family budgets, health and living standards are all affected by these issues in the long term. Surely these are things which rightfully concern their local District Councillor and a Party with aspirations of governing a country. However, they were long-term issues and Branch Meetings or Manifesto Committees all concentrating on the issues of today and/or the immediate election.

A paper on Adulterated Foods created some interest and a reprint in the Community Health Council Agenda, but none in the Party – despite a whole Christmas holiday given over to this, including Christmas Day.

Microwave ovens did not interest the Party either, but my comments via a letter to the press nearly brought a £100,000 writ!

My concern was because microwave ovens were very new and each new brand was leaps ahead of the previous one marketed by another manufacturer. Thus 'old' models were being ditched when only months old sometimes. 'For Sale' adverts in the local press told the story. '£300 model for only £30.'

Even if (if?) the original owner realised the need for regular servicing to pick up 'leaks' of microwaves from around doors, it was unlikely that the second (or third) owner was aware of this six-monthly need. My letter to the local press on this point was taken up by a regional newspaper (*The Mercury*) describing me as an 'Environmental Chief' (I was Chairman of the Warwickshire Environmental Protection Council at the time). This Sunday Regional coverage caused big trouble for microwave manufacturers and distributors. Their staff refused to start work on Monday morning. Hence one manufacturer threatened to sue me for £100,000 worth of lost sales that could occur over a period just when he was seeing light at the end of a long tunnel of investments, according to him.

Returning from a hard day on the factory floor to deal with a succession of such irate phone callers tends to get you a bit worried. I went down with a form of meningitis and lost three weeks off work. 'You wouldn't be in it if it wasn't for the money,' is the usual insult thrown at Councillors. What money when you are off work for three weeks with no pay?

Fortunately, the Warwickshire Protection Council came to my aid. The local Environmental Chief Officer took over all the inquiries answering them by reference to the Protection Councils suitably vague follow-up publication. For once my Ordinary National Certificate in Engineering and my Open University Degree proved helpful – apparently manufacturers are hesitant to challenge the opinions of 'scientists' in court!

Other interesting inquiries for information came from individuals countrywide and from such unlikely organisations as branches of the Ambulance Brigade and the Police Federation, who both used microwave ovens in their canteens. You never know who your friends are these days.

Also the Protection Council's recommendation to have a warning embossed on the front of each oven went forward to the EEC for their consideration when they draft regulations to cover the issue. (When?) I had suggested the embossed sign should read 'DANGER – MICROWAVES', but soon extra safety devices on new models negated the need for this. However, older models were still being used and sold on.

Leaving my allotments for the greater good may bring some benefit to someone in Europe. I hope so, because it was leaving me out of pocket – phone calls, letters replying to individuals all over the country, stationery and now three weeks' lost earnings. The telephone-answering service and typing provided free by my wife was considerable by now, and the inevitable disruption of family life was affecting my two children as I got more and more involved and bogged down with Councillor's duties. 'You're only in it for the money,' according to the bulk of the public. What money? Housekeeping money subsidising Councillor activities and me off sick relying on my wife's wages – there was no company-paid Sick Leave for manual workers such as myself.

Councillor's Allowances and Family Involvement

When first elected I was naive enough to think that Attendance Money for council meetings was a perk, i.e. money nice to have but not an essential part of the exercise. I even toyed with the idea of not claiming. However, I did ask several colleagues who were returning for a second or third spell what was the norm. I did not wish to rock the boat one way or the other if Party policy or Group tactics were involved.

There was no Party or Group policy – or norm, for that matter, no advice either. Some claimed consistently for all claimable items, that is advertised Surgeries (one per month), all Council meetings attended and for any Outside Body meetings if claims were allowed (very few allowed for Outside Bodies), plus travel expenses at laid-down rates for travel to and from all claimable occasions – which were very few in practice. If the duty was not claimable no travel expenses were entertained either. School Governorships, for example, were not claimable for Attendance Money or travel expenses. (Councillors, in committee, decide the amounts allowed and which bodies can be claimed for, therefore there is variation from Council to Council up and down the land.)

Some colleagues had a sliding scale of claims: full amount for meetings lasting (say) five hours and over, proportionally less for shorter meetings. Nothing for short Subcommittees, which coincided with passing by the Town Hall on the way home from work. Subcommittees tended to be held at 5 p.m. for this very reason.

Two colleagues with Public Service going way back to yesteryear did not claim anything at that time, still despising the 'paid' approach for public service.

I chose the staggered claim approach, arguing to myself that some money was warranted for lost overtime, which had always been available to me, extra telephone bills (unclaimable), stamps and stationery, etc. These, I reasoned, had to be paid for even if time and experience was given free in out-of-work hours. Some more progressive Councils allow claims for stamps, stationery and telephone bills.

I was very soon to change even this approach and start to claim full amounts for all meetings claimable, however long- or short-lasting. Indeed the two older colleagues who had given public service free for twenty years and more under the old Town Council system were to start claiming also for District duties. The outgoings, extra and deeper involvement and background work, investigations, studies and house calls, eventually convinced them that the electorate were getting their extended services cheaply whatever they claimed. I came to the same conclusion; indeed, I still needed to dip into the housekeeping money to meet my Council expenses and I used my wife as an unpaid secretary, of course.

The duties of a District Councillor and the time it requires is a considerable step up from that of the old Town Councillor of pre-1974 reorganisation era. It is no longer a position for the well-intentioned 'do-gooder'. Indeed the ever-present and very real threat of being surcharged at the District Auditors behest should he or she decide District Councillors have been negligent makes that point better than I can. Company Directors have no such threat hanging over their heads should their decisions prove inappropriate, ill-advised or unfortunate for the Company – yet they expect to get paid well for their services with added Company Shares and emoluments if the advice comes up trumps.

Much has been written, most of it derogatory, about a Councillor's worth – mostly by people who have no intention of ever putting in any public service. Their caustic and critical comments do a lot of harm by putting off others who might be considering public office and it also forces out of office many who would mature into experienced Councillors. The combination of such public attacks and the very low allowance available to Councillors can effectively keep the more able people from standing. Capable people can put their talent to a profession, career or business, where returns in both money and gratitude make a much more pleasant life for them and their families.

Had I realised this in advance I don't suppose I would ever have offered myself either, but at that time I too did not think it needed any particular talents or ability to be a Councillor. I was awarded an Open University Degree the very same week in which I was first elected; therefore, the public were not getting a pig in a poke – just a pig with a Degree. I was just as ignorant of the requirements and range of duties of a District Councillor as any other member of the public, therefore I cannot blame others for being equally uninformed.

Fortunately for local democracy there are still such people about like me who never came into contact with the problems and setbacks of holding public office until after being elected. It's too late to turn back then without losing face. I must emphasise, however, that I just did not realise the depth of antagonism there is towards people in public office; therefore I carried on believing attitudes would mellow, perhaps even become sympathetic in time. Those I did help became friends, but the great majority remain sceptical, ready and willing to criticise and blame – yet they offer no alternative. (Except the National Front members, perhaps?)

There may be others in public office who knew in

advance the insults they would be subjected to, and who still bashed on. They must be made of steel.

It is also most unfortunate that when a person gets elected to public office their families get the knocks as well, especially a spouse. Why a person is immediately regarded as mentally defective upon election beats me – why their spouse should be so regarded is even more bewildering. It can drive a spouse to ground, cause bitterness and resentfulness in families and even break up marriages. Local Government is threatened as a result. Not enough able people come forward, and why should they for this treatment and very little financial recompense to boot?

Financial allowances at any level could never compensate. The meagre allowances currently paid are an insult if looked at as compensation and they scarcely (if at all) cover the expense of office – extra telephone bills, stationery, petrol (not counting extra car repairs), and photocopying information for circulation on subjects under consideration.

My first year's allowances added up to £635 for Attendance Money, petrol to and from claimable meetings and rent for telephone; 35% was stopped as Income Tax, similarly NI contribution was stopped, so about £400 was actually received.

Still money in hand readers may think.

Not so!

For starters petrol had to be paid for before it could be claimed back less tax – nothing in hand for that. Telephone rent? More debatable because most (not all) Councillors would not be paying this anyway. But attendance money? At least that was something to cover the time spent at meetings.

Not so!

My telephone bill increased by £120 per year – and reduced by that amount immediately my councilloring ceased. So! There is still £280 pounds left to spend.

Not so!

The Outside Bodies meetings, Governor meetings, house calls, necessary supporting meetings – public meetings, forums/meetings on pertinent issues e.g. Group Meetings, all had to be travelled to and from. My extra petrol consumption was easily £5 per week extra (not counting wear and tear), i.e. £250 per year at a modest estimate for that petrol used over and above the refundable petrol.

Ah, but there is still £30 to 'piss up the wall' you all chorus.

Not so!

For a start that was claimed for petrol money spent to go to and from claimable meetings, and there are still stamps – at least £1 per month (£12) plus reams of typing paper (and a typewriter in the first year), carbon, envelopes, notepads. You are into the housekeeping money now.

Just why should I deprive my wife of housekeeping money to run a District for you? And what about this money 'for just attending meetings' as letters to the press always state insultingly when attacking Councillors. There is none left – but we still attended meetings, swotted up the Agendas over the weekend, investigated, checked out, rang colleagues for advice, called at sites, agencies, house calls as required to brief ourselves. Such is 'just attending meetings'.

Allowances are an insult if regarded as 'pay' for the hours of concentrated effort involved, albeit much of it mental effort required to match highly trained professional officers. All decisions, even delegated ones, are the responsibility of elected members. Officers implement them; they will not be surcharged for mistakes. No, sir! The stress and strain and responsibility is on the shoulders of the elected Councillors.

It is a situation recognised by the Government, hence the

Robinson Inquiry set up by the Government. The Robinson committee recommended £1,000 per year (1982) as set payment to each District Councillor irrespective of nature of office, whether in control or in opposition, plus the allowances claimable as appropriate on top. This was not implemented by the Government despite the findings of its own Inquiry.

It may be that readers in the know are thinking of the £1,000 and larger claims currently made by some existing Councillors.

Very big claims are usually made by County Councillors (or Metropolitan in large urban areas) and they will be attending daytime meetings, such is the importance of their duties. Thus £3,000, £4,000 or £5,000 claims are, in fact, loss of earnings – they are down that much in their salaries/pay packets, plus forfeiting promotion chances (several more thousands down). Some District Councils also meet during the daytime to accommodate Councillors from rural or island areas with long distances to travel to and from meetings. These will also have extra travel money in their claims making their Allowances look inflated even more when, in fact, it's returned money already spent on travel and in some cases overnight accommodation.

However, for more urban districts, evening meetings are the norm and very little loss of earnings is involved, probably none, because its an either/or method of claiming. So why the £1,000-plus claims? Why not £635 like mine?

Leading members of controlling groups have to put in many more sessions with officers (for example) both as Chairman of Committee and sitting on many more Subcommittees, Committees, Planning Forums, etc., than opposition members. Opposition members were not expected or welcome at many such meetings. Just what my workload would have been if I had been a member of the Controlling Group I shudder to think!

MR George.
Sec/Sol:
  Do I have to Declare an Interest on Items (2 on Agenda) which threaten to use my 2 plots (£1 Rent each) for Housing?

Hughie Griffiths

This is a difficult one! I am inclined to think you would be well advised to declare an interest. I could, if you so wish, seek a dispensation from the Sec of State but I could not get this by the date of the Council meeting.

Notes exchanged during my first Council Meeting. The Sec: of State did not grant the dispensation – then or later. H.G.

Notes passed in Council meeting on declaring an interest

Labour lash Tory treatment

New member of Warwick District Council, Coun Hugh Griffiths, is "furious" at the treatment meeted out to him by the Conservative chairman of a housing sub-committee.

Coun Griffiths told the CP yesterday that he had been told to leave the previous evening's meeting of the housing management sub-committee. Although he is not a member of the committee he had just wished to sit and listen.

He said: "At the first break in proceedings my presence was challenged by the chairman (Coun John Wilson) under his interpretation of Standing Orders and I was asked to leave."

Coun Griffiths, who represents Crown Ward, said he was very much concerned with the problems of council house tenants and had felt as a "new boy" it would be helpful for him to listen to the committee's discussions.

He added: "I am furious. It's very difficult to see how I can adequately represent Crown Ward when I am told to leave meetings and even debates in full council are being given the guillotine."

Labour group leader, Coun Peter Tombs, said they intended raising the matter. He said it was the second time that a Labour member had been told to leave the meeting of this sub-committee.

20. *Lillington C.E.First School*
    1. Cllr.WILLIAMS
    2. Cllr.MRS.WEARE

21. *Lillington Middle School*
    1. Cllr.WILLIAMS
    2. Cllr.CHARLES
    ✷ 3. Cllr.GRIFFITHS

22. *Milverton Combined School*
    1. Cllr.MRS.BULL
    2. Cllr.COX
    ✷ 3. Cllr.GRIFFITHS

23. *Whitnash Combined School*
    1. Cllr.MANN
    2. Cllr.KIRTON

24. *Nursery Schools*
    (A) *Kenilworth & Warwick*
    1. Cllr.MRS.CHANDLEY
    (B) *Lillington & Whitnash*
    2. Cllr.MANN

25. *Warwick St.Michael's Day School*
    1. Cllr.MRS.CHANDLEY

26. *Gresham Day Special School, L/Spa*
    1. Cllr.WILKINS
    2. Cllr.MANN

27. *Millbrook Grange Special School, Kenilworth*
    1. Cllr.HARRISON

28. *Warwick Hospital Special School & Ridgeway Day Special School*
    1. Cllr.BUTLER

29. *Mid-Warwickshire College of F.E.*
    1. Cllr.BOXLEY
    2. Cllr.G.W.C.WILSON
    3. Cllr.THOMAS

30. *County Education Committee*
    1. Cllr.KERRY

Other Organisations (1982-1983)

31. *Warwickshire Branch Assoc.of District Councils*
    1. Cllr.HIGGINS
    2. Cllr.RAWNSLEY
    3. Cllr.WOZENCROFT

32. *Warwickshire Computer Management Board*
    1. Cllr.HIGGINS

33. *Planning & Transportation Local Consultative Committee*
    1. Cllr.BARTON
    2. Cllr.KERRY
    3. Cllr.MANN
    4. Cllr.MORLEY
    5. Cllr.McAUSLAN

34. *West Midlands Regional Health Authority - Community Health Council (to 31.8.82)*
    1. Cllr.SIMPSON
    2. Cllr.MONNINGTON
    ✷ 3. Cllr.GRIFFITHS
    4. Cllr.WILKINS
    5. Cllr.BUTLER
    6. Cllr.CLEAVER

35. *Warwickshire Environmental Protection Council*
    1. Cllr.MRS.BULL
    ✷ 2. Cllr.GRIFFITHS
    3. Cllr.MRS.WEARE
    Reserve Members:
    4. Cllr.TILDEN-SMITH
    5. Cllr.McAUSLAN

36. *Warwick District Safety Committee*
    1. Cllr.MRS.BULL
    2. Cllr.WILLIAMS
    3. Cllr.ACTON
    4. Cllr.T̶H̶O̶M̶A̶S̶
    5. Cllr.THURLOW
    6. Cllr.KIRTON

    Cllr.Wendybank Jan 13

Extracts from Warwick District Council's Year Book 1982/83

68. *Netherfield Management Committee (Formerly known as Dale Street Day Centre Management Cttee.,L/Spa)*
   1. Cllr.MRS.BULL
   2. Cllr.WILLIAMS
   3. Cllr.MRS.WEARE

69. *South Warwickshire Group Homes Association*
   1. Cllr.MRS.WEARE

70. *Bath Place Community Venture & Management Committee*
   1. Cllr.WALKER
   2. Cllr.COX
   3. Cllr.MS.E.MORRIS

71. *Family Practitioner Committee*
   1. Cllr.ROWLEY

72. *Birmingham Airport Consultative Committee*
   1. Cllr.KIMPTON

73. *South Warwickshire Marriage Guidance Council Executive Committee*
   ✳ 1. Cllr.GRIFFITHS

74. *Lapworth Charity*
   1. Cllr.KIMPTON

75. *West Midlands Art*
   1. Chairman of the Recreation & Amenities Committee or nominee.

76. *Post Office Advisory Committee*
   1. Cllr.RAWNSLEY

77. *Heathcote Executive Committee*
   1. Cllr.BARTON
   2. Cllr.MANN
   3. Cllr.PARKER
   4. Cllr.HOWLETT
   5. Cllr.STOCKTON

78. *Coventry Independent Local Radio Advisory Committee*
   1. Cllr.RAWNSLEY

79. *Thomas Oken's and Nicholas Eyffler's Charity*
   1. Cllr.MRS.CHANDLEY

80. *Sydenham Community Association Management Committee*
   1. Cllr.PARKER
   2. Cllr.BYRD

81. *South Warks.Area Health Authority*
   1. Cllr.J.M.MORRIS

82. *West Midlands Regional Planning Authorities Conference*
   1. Cllr.MORLEY

Up to six councillors needed on some of the eighty-two outside bodies

Cllr. Griffith No. 12

Memo Pad Breakdown
From 9/7/80 to 29/9/80,
ie during a "holiday" period! (Holiday for who?)

```
         HOUSING DEP'T      27
         R/AMENITIES         2
         EN: HEALTH          1
         PLAN' + TECH'       6
CHIEF EX:/SOLICITOR          2
         OTHERS              7
                            ―――
                            45  (43 Cases)
REPEAT (CHASING UP) MEMOS    5
                            ―――
                            50
```

Breakdown of cases in a typical Memo Pad.

THE South Warwickshire Marriage Guidance Council is available to deal with problems in any relationship — a marriage certificate is not needed to get an appointment.

That was the message from the council this week which is now trying to project a more "down-to-earth" image, according to the executive committee's press officer Coun Hughie Griffiths.

Between January and June the council dealt with 108 first appointments, and 378 subsequent appointments which included 42 single women and 14 single men. A total of 198 children under the age of 16 were involved.

Highlighting the number of single people coming for help, Coun Griffiths said: "This demonstrates that we deal with any relationship problem.

By HELEN PENRICE

Single

"Marriage guidance is becoming a bit of a misnomer. We are also trying to get away from the snooty middle class image of yesteryear which gave the impression that a marriage certificate was a pre-requisite to an appointment."

He also emphasises they the council does not only deal with male-female relationships.

"They could be mother and older daughters or older stay-at-home sons. They may not be a blood tie but perhaps a lodger/landlady relationship of long-standing, or friends and flatmates," said Coun Griffiths.

He also said an increasing number of single people were coming not because they had a relationship but because they cannot make a lasting relationship.

There is a growing trend for counsellors to be seconded to doctors' surgeries.

"Chats with a counsellor can often eliminate the cause of stress and thereby the illness without the use of expensive drugs," said Coun Griffiths.

"We need to get out new meet-the-people down-to-earth image across to the public and want to smash down the barriers.

Coun Griffiths also reports that the move to better premises next door at 35 Regent Grove has been delayed. It has still to be approved by the district council's land and buildings sub-committee.

He said: "We are all disappointed at the delay but great things are expected once we have moved into better premises."

The Southwark Warwickshire Marriage Guidance press release

Residents hope for end to nightmare

RESIDENTS of Marston Close in Lillington are delighted that after a two-year battle the district council is now doing something about their flats which have been described as a "nightmare."

But at last week's council meeting a row about who was to blame for construction problems at the flats broke out.

Councillors alternately blamed building inspectors, the architects and the tenants themselves.

Tenants protests over the past two years — mainly about damp and noise — have included threatened rent strikes and a demonstration. This involved some of them carrying mouldy clothes right to the front door of housing committee chairman, Coun Roy Charles.

Measures now being taken to cure the problems include cavity filling of the structural walls, installation of suspended ceilings or alternative flooring, central heating and the securing of upper-storey doors.

And in an attempt to reduce the noise problem, the council is now using an unoccupied flat to experiment with different sound proofing methods.

Residents' association secretary Mrs Brenda Arnold, said they were delighted that action was now being taken.

Normally

"They are lovely flats but we'll be a lot happier when the council has done something about the sound proofing," she said. This is the biggest remaining problem, she added.

Mrs Hilary Wakeling of No 19 said her family had to take off their shoes because the people in the flat below can hear them moving around.

"We cannot live normally because we are afraid of making a noise," she said.

Last week Labour's Coun Hughie Griffiths told the council: "A lot of this should never have happened if there had been adequate and proper inspection of the property at the time of building."

"This is a public building which cost hundreds of thousands of pounds to construct and hopefully will last 60 years," said Coun John Benyon (Lab). "But it has caused a great deal of suffering to the people who live there and has been a waste of public money.

"Councillors should be appalled at what has happened to Marston Close and we should keep a very careful eye on it and should scrutinise the building of our council houses."

But Coun Bernard Kirton (Ratepayer) said it was not the fault of the building-inspector's but the fault of the architects who designed the flats.

Absence

And Coun Bob Butler (Lib) said that damp in a lot of cases was the fault of the people who lived in the property. They used Calor gas heating and put polystyrene tiles on walls and ceilings, he said, making the rooms like hot houses.

Coun Charles said that at the time Marston Close was being built, one of the clerks of work was taken suddenly very ill.

There are few enough clerks anyway, and the absence of one made things more difficult, he said.

Mouldy flats getting the full treatment

A NEW experiment to combat the problems of condensation and mould growth in council flats has just been launched in Lillington.

The problems have plagued council tenants for some years now, especially in the high rise flats in Lillington in Leamington.

Particularly badly affected are the 14-storey Eden Court building and its two slightly lower neighbours, Ashton Court and Southorn Court.

In an attempt to tackle the problem the council is conducting an experiment in co-operation with the East Midlands Electricity Board at two flats in Ashton Court.

During the last couple of months the council has insulated the outside walls of the flats with a mixture of polystyrene and plaster. In addition, the inside walls have been treated with a chemical to combat mould growth.

The electricity board has installed new storage heaters in each room in the flat and an extractor fan has been put in the kitchens.

District council housing manager Mr Cecil Bradshaw says the flats will be monitored throughout the winter to see if the new installations solve the problem. He would be reporting back to the housing management sub-committee next spring.

All the flats currently have under-floor central heating but Mr Bradshaw says it is not going to be effective much longer.

So the storage heating is being considered as a replacement for the out-dated heating which is nearly 20 years old.

One of the people who led the campaign by tenants to get the council to do something about the problems was Mr Robert Boad of 78 Ashton Court.

TESTING

Mr Boad, who is chairman of the Lillington Tenants' Association, lives in one of the flats in which the experiment is being carried out.

"If this does not work I don't know what else will work," said Mr Boad.

The housing department has also been tackling similar problems in Marston Close, Lillington. Extra central heating has been installed in council property and insulation measures are also being planned.

Family fear eviction will split them up

A move to escape from the violent streets of London could lead to eviction for a young family now living in Lillington.

Mrs Sue Still, aged 20, and her husband Mick, 21 and their two-year-old daughther Nicola moved to the area 18 months ago from a Kensington Housing Trust Flat in London.

Mrs Still, three months pregnant said life in London was intolerable, so the family moved here to stay with her mother in a council flat at Warwick.

From there they moved to a top floor flat in Mason Avenue, Lillington — and now they face eviction on August 12, despite appeals to the district council, housing associations and private landlords.

The couple have lived there for seven months. The council could let them stay for up to 12 months under licence but, the Stills must be out by August 12.

Said Mrs Still: "We are getting desperate because we just have nowhere to go. Mick is unemployed so we can't afford a deposit for a place of our own.

"We have contacted all the housing associations locally and are on all their lists. We have also tried private accommodation but landlords will not have children.

"I am terrified this will split the family and the council may put Nicola into care. This business has put the whole family under a lot of strain."

But the case has angered Labour councillor Hughie Griffiths

"This family have been model occupiers. They are not in arrears and have never caused any trouble. They are a delightful couple and have tried their hardest to find alternative accommodation.

"It strikes me that here is a family who need a break who have pulled their weight and have got kicked in the teeth for it by a housing committee that is inconsistent, and heartless. I find it quite disgraceful."

And Coun Griffiths said: "I am prepared to support the Stills through thick and thin." He hopes to get the housing committee to reconsider the case.

Housing officer Mr Cecil Bradshaw said the council had fulfilled its obligation to house the family under the Housing (Homeless Person) Act 1977, and could do no more.

He said because the Stills moved from London to Warwick with no accommodation planned, they had made themselves homeless.

He said: "The Stills had a tenancy in London which they gave up. They were considered then to be intentionally homeless and that situation has not changed."

Eviction threat family saved by flat offer

By BRIAN RICHARDSON

A YOUNG Leamington couple's battle against eviction and homelessness has finally ended happily. With only two weeks to go before bailiffs were due to evict them from their council flat the Still family have been offered alternative accommodation.

Now instead of the prospect of life on the streets and the break-up of the family Mick Still, his pregnant wife Sue and their two-year-old daughter Nichola are looking forward to living in a modern flat on the Sydenham estate.

Classed

The Stills were granted a top-floor council flat at 107 Mason Avenue, Lillington, when they moved into the area from London last December.

Originally the council said they could stay for only three months but later extended the limit to August 12.

However, because the council classed the Stills as intentionally homeless they were adamant that they would have to move before 12 months elapsed and they became secure tenants.

When the first deadline expired without the Stills moving the council obtained a court order giving the family until November 1 to leave.

But with time rapidly running out a local housing association finally came to the rescue with the offer of the Sydenham flat.

"We've been saved at the last moment," said Mrs Still. "It has been a terrible strain over the last couple of months. Now I can look forward to a new home in time for my 21st birthday and the arrival of the baby in February.

Move

"We're so grateful to the councillors and those who signed and organised the petitions supporting us. We would have been made homeless without their efforts."

The Stills will move into their new home on November 7 and are being allowed to remain in the Mason Avenue flat until then.

The family had been on the housing association's books for almost three years.

Unemployed urged to quit area

UNEMPLOYED people in mid-Warwickshire should be encouraged to leave the area, says a Leamington councillor.

He is urging families hit by poor housing and unemployment to start afresh in Northampton, which is taking overspill population.

Councillor Hugh Griffiths has contacted the Northampton Development Corporation, urging them to flood Leamington employment exchange and housing department with leaflets promoting the town.

Coun. Griffiths represents Lillington's Crown ward on Warwick District Council and said his ward suffered particularly from the shortage of housing and jobs.

He has offered to co-operate with the development corporation in promoting Northampton among his constituents.

"It is not an easy task to persuade people to move even short distances," he admitted: "We can but try."

"There are 2,577 people unemployed in this area, plus 2,400 families on the housing waiting list, 800 in urgent need.

"One can guess why I am trying to relieve the situation by suggesting Northampton as an alternative."

Coun. Griffiths said he had received leaflets from Northampton on subsistence grants and moving expenses available to families moving into the area.

He understood job opportunities were abundant and new houses available. Northampton was only a short distance away and people making the move would be able to keep in touch with Leamington.

Spa sitting on rich coal seam

NCB STATEMENT URGED

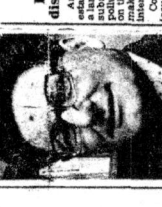

BY BRUCE HARRISON

Leamington is sitting on one of the biggest coalfields ever discovered in Britain, says Coun Hughie Griffiths.

And, fearing that the establishment in the district of large-scale mining may lead to subsidence, dust and air pollution, he yesterday called on the National Coal Board to make an early statement of intent about the plans.

Coun Hughie Griffiths is issuing to fellow Labour members of the district council a seven-page report on the prospects for the area, if the Coal Board decides to mine big, thick seam for which extensive boreholes have already been drilled.

He forecasts that the seam is between seven and ten feet thick and that it runs deep right through the district.

"Centred on Kenilworth, the local seam covers a huge part of Warwick district," he says. "My estimate of current drilling operations in this area is about 200 square miles, and still expanding as the south-western fringes are sought in the Wellesbourne area.

"It has been variously described by the NCB as two and a half times as big as the Nottingham Belvoir Dale field (the previous largest discovery in Britain) and belonging to a seam running from Nottingham to the south coast."

Coun Griffiths' report compares the mining of this coal with that at Selby, York-shire, and says: "If coal mining of this magnitude is to come to the Warwick district I feel the NCB should be pressured for an early statement of intent so that forward planning can take account of the problems.

"For example, should the route of the M40 be over this seam? Should houses be built on concrete rafts to lessen the effects of subsidence? Indeed, should large-scale development such as the Heathcote proposals go ahead at all?

"Should drains and sewers be laid with steeper gradients to lessen the risk of backflows after subsidence? Where structures have to be built — bridges, roads, buildings — should flexible joints be used as far as possible?"

He says the NCB will use its advanced technology to mine Warwickshire's coal if and when it decides to do so. Coal mining here will be a large-scale operation.

Coun Hughie Griffiths, a machine shop inspector at AP, has a family mining background, which has made him interested in the subject. He gained an Open University degree in sociology two years ago, having in the previous 16 years gained extensive engineering qualifications.

Councillors' allowances 'inadequate'

The attendance money paid to members of Warwick District Council is inadequate, whatever the press, the public or the Liberals may have to say, Coun Hughie Griffiths (Lab) told the Finance sub-committee.

When he received £400 at the end of the year it might seem a lot to some people. But if they thought it was easy money there would be no shortage of candidates.

The allowances were taxed, and members earned it not only because of the hours they put in at meetings, but the time spent studying the minutes.

"I lose £20 earnings a day to go to the Protection committee and then I have to pay for petrol, stationery and stamps," he said. "There are many meetings we can't claim for.

DIVORCE

"When I get money I try to buy something for the kitchen. It is the only way I can avoid a divorce.

"It is the poorest pay I have ever worked for, and I am one of the lower paid fraternity. Vets charge £18 an hour for their services. We seldom make more than £12 a week from one meeting."

It was agreed to refer to the Policy and Resources committee a recommendation that attendance allowances be raised from £12.14 for each period of 24 hours to £13. The national rate is now £14.

Coun Kenneth Rawnsley, Conservative group leader, suggested the figure of £13, but Coun Peter Byrd (Lab), said members should receive the full £14. Some members, he said, needed the money. "I don't think we should feel at all coy about claiming it," he said.

Coun Miss Estelle Morris (Lab) said it was intolerable that members had to negotiate their own salary increases each year.

Coun John Wilson (Con) said that while recognising that members were underpaid they should set an example.

Not a do-gooder's job

So Mr Elms 13.4.81) thinks I should count myself lucky to be able to afford to represent him at District Council meetings and asks what training have I had?

It so happens that I think newly-elected district councillors should receive some training. It's a very daunting experience speaking in the Chamber. Asides and hubbub is the reception my attempts are greeted with. No different, of course, to any broadcast from Parliament, but very nerve-racking to the one on the receiving end — as it is designed to be by your opponents. In my opinion this is why about 50 per cent of elected members never speak in full council, and seldom stand again as councillors.

However, there is formal training and training via experience. People should not offer themselves as candidates unless they are involved with the society around them, and therefore are a fair reflection of the area they represent. Thus actual occupations or professions and years of unpaid voluntary work and meetings help make a councillor. This doubles and trebles once elected. Standing vacancies on 51 outside bodies on top of governorships of 30 local schools have to be filled at the very first council AGM — several places on each body. Related activities are expected of any such appointed member of governor — most of them involving sponsorship — even church 'parades' expect collections.

Meanwhile a councillor's spouse and family at home are not only unpaid secretary and typist and telephone answering service for the two and a half constituency cases I average per week, but are deprived of one's company; wait a generation for odd jobs to be done, and have all the upsets that go with council duties. They are usually at home alone to take the abusive phone calls, the heavy-breathers and the callers who ask if that is the councillor's home — leaving everyone guessing as to their intentions. A bomb perhaps! Phone calls at 12.30, 1.30, 4.10, 6.00 am disturb the whole household — paid or otherwise, and all of us have to be at work on time the next morning or risk the sack like anyone else. I have been suspended for three days for losing time for a daytime school function. Such 'treatment' can go on for 20-30 years of public life (some life!). Is it too much to buy a kitchen item for a long-suffering wife Mr Elms?

However, it was even more weighty matters which prompted my statement that councillors' attendance money was inadequate.

Duties at district level is not a job for well-intentioned do-gooders. It needs a body of representatives whose combined experience and professional capabilities are up to the tasks. For example councillors are employer of over 900 — one of the largest employers in the area; they are landlord to a vast acreage of land over and above the 200 acres under parks and gardens control; they are landlord for over 8,000 houses with all the repair and maintenance problems that entails, and for 1,000 or so commercial premises — mostly shops, bringing a number of legal problems; the recreational facilities, three swimming pools, tennis courts, bowling greens, golf courses, pitches of all types and accompanying changing rooms, fishing rights — you name it, we have to administer it according to laws and by-laws and to the public's satisfaction.

Add environment, conservation, planning (from dropped kerbs to multi-million pound developments), roads footpaths, pavements and accompanying drains and you can see why the council's turnover adds up to £17m per year, with a capital expenditure of over £3m a year and a £38m ongoing debt to be serviced. Where do you get the expertise to ensure the cheapest money is borrowed at £14 a meeting, Mr Elms? Our officers are good — but they are not answerable. The councillors are, the District Auditor surcharges councillors for any mistakes made.

District councillors, like others, all do their best. We do bring a wide range of professional knowledge, job experience and background studies with us and we try and train ourselves as we go along. I obtained my first (of eleven) 'O' levels at 35 and a degree at 45 — at my own expense and with the loss of night shift earnings when attending evening classes. With experience on varied jobs, gardening/roundsman/ building (registered plumber), engineering (ONC) I feel I have done my best to get "trained" for the duties as a district councillor — no less so than any vet or similar professional person.

There are, of course, members with Doctorates, one professor, and similar qualifications — and they are all equally busy people with family commitments. However, I still think that the public will only get what it is prepared to pay for, be it in education standards, council services or councillors. It is not a do gooder's job.

If you want the job doing better, as constituents are always pressing for, then pay a reasonable attendance allowance to attract the Master Minds (if there are any others!) or to compensate the families of those who struggle like me. — H. Griffiths BA, Crown Ward Councillor (Cubbington and Radford County Council Candidate), 23 Kenilworth Road, Cubbington.

Councillor's wife abused by phone

Councillors earn their attendance money if only for the abuse they have to stand, Coun Hughie Griffiths (Lab) told the district Policy and Resources committee.

The Government now permits a maximum of £14 in any one day for attendance at council, committee or sub-committee meetings, and £14 for surgeries or meetings between committee chairmen or party leaders and chief officers.

This compares with the district council's present £12 and £5. Coun John Higgins, Finance sub-committee chairman, suggested increases to £13 and £6.

Coun Roger Mann (Con) proposed that the full Government allowance be allowed.

Whether members claimed was a matter of conscience, but if a member needed the money he should be entitled to it. There were many who did not.

Coun Griffiths said he would be one who would claim.

"At work I can't wash my hands, but I am abused and told I am idle and useless and spending ratepayers' money by the million," he said.

"We have a turnover of £17 million, capital expenditure of more than £3 million a year and we have to service £38 million. Where do you get the expertise for £12, £13 or even £14 a meeting?"

MASTERMINDS

Coun Griffiths said his wife and family had been abused by telephone and there had even been heavy breathers.

The pay was nothing like enough to attract masterminds to be councillors.

Coun Kenneth Rawnsley (chairman): "I take it you are not prepared to kill the cock that lays the golden eggs."

Councillors had a duty to the ratepayers and the country to show they were not necessarily going to grab everything they could get their hands on, said Coun Michael Coker (Con). They should show responsibility, as many other people had done.

Coun Chris Clark (Con) said members should not be hindered in their work with worries about financial problems.

The maximum £14 was approved by ten votes to eight.

The committee agreed to a recommendation by Labour leader Coun Brian Weekes that the Selection committee be asked to consider whether there was an automatic way in which allowances could be determined in future.

Coun James Whitby (Con) said members should not be allowed to claim for adjourned council meetings, which were caused by lengthy speeches, mostly repetitive.

"I don't see why ratepayers should pay for repetition," he said.

Councillor Hughie's fan club

● My own personal experience of Hughie, as Coun Griffiths likes to be called, is that he is one of the working councillors who is dedicated to the job he was elected for by the residents in this ward.

I won't go into details of my problem, but I will say one thing: only for Hughie coming to my previous address at 2 am, my wife and I would now be in Hatton or our graves.

I would like to point out to those people who think councillors don't earn their £12 that I and many more say they do.

They should get a rise, also loss of earnings, travelling expenses and, last but not least, extra for being called upon at all times, the same as any other professional bodies dedicated to their jobs. I make this statement for one reason. We are a small congregation of people who are doing a service, such as councillors, shop stewards and other unpaid bodies and I say good luck to all, and keep it up — including Hughie. — **G. F. Owen, Chairman TGWU 5/620, 4 Shuckburgh Grove, Lillington.**

● A word in defence of Coun Hughie Griffiths. I was surprised to read the attacks on Hughie, and to say he is not worth his salt is unwarranted.

Crown Way car park on Saturday — Coun Griffiths is there, ready and willing to meet people with their problems, and he does really take people's problems seriously. He is always ready and willing to help at any time, day or night. "Only a phone call away" is his motto; to say that one only sees him at election time is downright slush.

So less criticism of Coun Griffiths and a little more thank you and good wishes to him. — **D. Kirwan, 9 Hanworth Close, Lillington.**

● I really must say that I have been disgusted by the two correspondents who accuse Coun Griffiths of not being up to scratch.

We certainly want him to stand again, whatever he claims as attendance money. It's small indeed for the help he gives. For many years I nursed a sick husband and he had a serious operation. Coun Griffiths has taken up several problems for us — house repairs and getting a written apology from a stand-in doctor who was rude to my daughter who was very ill.

We had to phone Coun Griffiths one night at 9.30 pm as we could not open the front or back doors as they were jammed tight as the council would surely attend to them sooner or later. Coun Griffiths came and had to push both doors from the outside as neither my husband nor I had the strength to open them from the inside. My husband's nerves were very bad and if the house caught fire we could not get out. Coun Griffiths went back home immediately and brought back a plane and eased the doors and talked to my husband to settle him down, then left for home around midnight.

Coun Griffiths helped us to get this sheltered accommodation and we are very pleased and happy with it. It's a big relief to me to have a warden you can call if my husband ever gets bad.

What more of Coun Griffiths do people want? They only have to contact him day or night. What a pity they abuse him and his wife so. — **Fair Play (Name and address supplied).**

Letters

A councillor and a friend

With reference to the recent letters, writing that Coun Griffiths is not worth his salt.

As a home help I visit a number of OAPs in his ward and they speak highly of him. For example, he answered a 4 am phone call from one OAP and later a New Year's Eve call with immediate visits to the old lady to give advice and comfort. He called the police to sort out her noisy neighbour problems and subsequently attended a case study get together with social workers, in his working hours, but unpaid, of course. He continued to call, advise, write letters and was always available when needed by the OAP, neighbours and myself.

The situation was finally resolved much to everyone's relief, but only after two years of hell for everyone concerned, including Coun Griffiths. Also not forgetting his wife, who on one occasion was deprived of his company during a festive season when the likes of you and I were out celebrating with our husbands and wives, family and friends.

To conclude, I think it is very unfair for people who have not had contact with Coun Griffiths to say he is not worth his salt.

Surely it is only just and proper to meet the man first, see his total commitment to his work and listen to his views before comments are made on his character.

Not worth his salt? I and many others who have befriended him have found him to be the salt of the earth. — **Mrs S. J. Beynon, 18 Thursfield Road, Leamington.**

Lament for Hughie . . .

Your item in the issue of October 27 "Councillor Griffiths blow for poll hopes" prompted the following:

Oh dear; Hughie, what have you done
To deserve such a vicious kick up the . . . . ?
All the years of service that you have given,
And the Party causes for which you have striven
Are all snuffed out like a candle light.
Did you do something Right?

J. R. A. Hardy, 72 Dunblane Drive, Leamington.

Unfair to Coun Hughie

I am surprised to read in your letters column of Coun Griffiths being attacked. This is most unwarranted. You can find him or his colleagues in the Crown Way car park every Saturday morning, whatever the weather. I see him every month at his monthly indoor surgery at the community centre in Mason Avenue. Indeed, I understand he pays the hiring fee, collects the keys, and opens up on most occasions. No problems are too large or small, for his attention, although many are persistent and cannot be solved easily.

However, few people take the trouble to call and see him, preferring to sit at home complaining. How can he know their problems if they do not take advantage of his surgeries.

It may take time, Town Halls being what they are — time wasters. I have had my housing and related problems attended to by him. Please let's have a 'thank you' or two, not this onslaught. It is most unfair. — **T. R. Green, Leamington.**

However, my involvement was such that I came to claim the full amounts possible however long or short a meeting – and one Full Council meeting lasted from 6 p.m. to 1.10 a.m. – and I still had to clock in that morning at 7.30 a.m. or risk the sack like any other manual worker.

I came to consider my involvement at meetings as an important part of running a large enterprise, the services of a District for 114,000 people. Ensuring the efficient operation of such services needed a lot of decisions, and they had to be right. Surcharges could bankrupt even quite well-off Councillors. They would put a working man on, or below, the breadline. His house, furniture and personal possessions could, and would, be sold over his head to make the payments and the balance settled by sending him/her to prison. To avoid any possibility of this a Councillor must put in a lot of effort and time ensuring his/her decisions are right. Indeed he/she must ensure correct decisions are made in order to get elected next time, and the next, and the next. Even a whisper of a scandal or misjudgement could have disastrous effects at election time.

It is not just a question of reading through Agenda papers, themselves lengthy Officer reports in many cases, but County Structure plans (twenty- or thirty-page booklets) have to be mastered and understood, likewise Housing Surveys for the whole District's housing, private as well as Council-owned. Long-term housing necessitates in-depth studies of employment prospects, commuter trends, local travel to work patterns, lorry routes in and out of the county and their likely effects on the District and, not least, servicing a £38 million debt to pay for such things (i.e. £105 million turnover) to be authorised in a manner that will pass District Auditor scrutiny. The methods and variations, plus the numerous sources, to borrow money yet keep within Central Government guidelines are seemingly infinite.

There are Heavy Metal in Air surveys; outbreaks of food poisoning reports; Development of the River's Upper Reaches reports; reports from nutters who want to build Superdromes for every craze from roller skating to health and beauty 'treatment', plus car rallies on Grand Prix scale around town... so on and so forth. All 'Reports' (booklets) have to be carefully studied especially if you are going to throw the ideas out. To provisionally accept at least gives you a little more time to assimilate the idea. In any event the on-going serious Officer Reports have to be decided upon so that Officers can proceed to drawing up plans (projections), estimates as the case may be, or not waste any more time on a project if it's a non-starter.

In addition it is necessary to master such financially complicated items as leasing arrangements for Council vehicles and plants – even leasing such unlikely items as major parts of new swimming pools to avoid breaking Central Government restrictions on Capital Expenditure. (Maggie was not having it all her own way in even Tory held Councils!) At the other end of the scale, Dustmen's carrying distances, access to properties, types of vehicles used, size of rounds, turning points at specific pick-up points, arranging collections over bank holidays – all such problems must be studied and decided upon so that Officers can issue appropriate instructions (and hide behind Councillors' decisions when the complaints flow in.)

In the same way Councillors have to decide on the one hand whether to pipe mains water to isolated dwellings, at great expense, and whether to update the sewage system for such properties or continue night soil collections at even greater costs.

In between such extremes are the making and/or enforcing of by-laws for keeping pets or wild animals, control of dogs in public places, vermin infestations, stubble burning, tombstones and kerbing or non-kerbing of graves, keeping or diverting footpaths – you name it, Councillors have to know all about it and be able to defend their arrangements and by-laws when petitions or individual complaints come in – as they do regularly.

On top of such complaints are a steady stream of annual complaints about non-collection of autumn leaves, blocked drain gulleys, inadequate grass cutting and similar items. From time to time you receive letters for or against wider issues such as teachers' pay, school class numbers and even school holidays not coinciding with the main factory holidays – issues you are drawn into as Councillor or Governor even though it is County Council business. There are also letters and circulars from businessmen either promoting or complaining about extensions or developments affecting their business. It is all Councillors' fault one way or another – hence the bad press Councillors get. No one points out the resulting chaos that would occur on a very wide front without the control brought about by Councillors. In fact, life would be impossible, hence Local Government was instigated some 150 years ago.

All these issues must be studied in your own time at home in preparation for debates and decision-taking in meetings. Even then it is not always possible to find a consensus of opinion even after debate. Further study and further debate is needed. Yet such repeat efforts only serve to annoy the public. Irrespective of such time-consuming attempts to get it right on behalf of the electorate, the best a Councillor can expect in return are public insults along the lines of, 'You are only in it for the money,' to your face, and, 'Why should Councillors get allowances for just attending meetings?' in letters to the press – with editorials to match such insults.

I repeat, public service is no longer a do-gooder's job nor a job for the faint hearted or slow on the uptake.

The range of services covered are very wide – much

wider than for professional Council Officers even (with the exception of the Chief Executive or equivalent). Officers specialise in their particular department's activities: Planning Officers – planning and its control; Environmental Health Officers – control of the environment generally, animals, slaughter houses, pets, harmful insects, epidemics, food poisoning, catering establishments, hotels and so forth; Recreation/Amenities Officers – public gardens, grassed areas, swimming baths/pools, play areas, parks and park facilities and so forth; Housing Officers – housing, dwellings and some council-owned shopping and commercial premises. A certain amount of overlap exists and Chief Officers and their deputies are expected to be conversant with other departments' activities. Indeed the modern Corporate Management Committee style dictates that a Chief Officer's Management team meets regularly (weekly) to ensure each department is briefed as fully as possible on the full range of Council activities and Council's decisions and requirements, and to eliminate duplication/double purchasing/idle plant/underused personnel/equipment, among other things. Such senior officers are time-served people with many years of experience probably gained with two or three different councils over a twenty- or thirty-year period coming through the lower grades.

As for an elected councillor, he finds himself on committees he had probably never heard of, still less gained years of experience in junior posts. Furthermore, from time to time a councillor will be switched across to other committees depending on the fortunes of elections or the need to strengthen (or otherwise) this or that committee. Thus even a Committee Chairman, by now with some specialist knowledge obtained in that position, can be switched to chair another committee at the behest of a Group decision. Any chairman, new or experienced, would be expected to go over Agenda papers before a meeting with 'his' or 'her' Chief Officer and match that Officer's grasp of the subject matter and in turn carry that understanding into the meeting in order to control the meeting. Officers have no control once the meeting starts – they can only advise when called upon to do so.

Officers spend a lifetime getting to grips with their department's needs and even then have been known to be ineffective, make mistakes or even fail to grasp situations. Only by arduous studying of Officers' reports, carefully following debates, plus pre-committee discussions with Officers, can a Chairman of a committee hope to avoid being ineffective in committee and thus avoid letting the public down.

I labour the point to establish in readers' minds that at least a certain portion of elected Councillors at District, County and Metropolitan levels must be prepared, capable and have the time to get very involved if the public are to have any control via the ballot box.

There was an alternative – in Russia!

Just why is all this time and mental effort needed? 'There is too much Government anyway,' you are all saying.

After being attacked in the press by members of the public after I had spoken in Council justifying my worth, I did itemise in a reply some of the services covered – but in seven years I could not hope to come to grips with them all, of course. One of the problems a Councillor (and officers) has is getting the range of services known. They are often run so smoothly in an ongoing manner that the public just do not notice them. Thus, in ignorance, people state, 'I can do my own Councilloring.' But have they ever stopped to consider that, in 1982 for example, Warwick District Councillors were the employer of over 9,000 – one of the largest employers in the area; they were landlord to a vast acreage of land over and above the 200 acres under Parks and Garden control; they were landlord for over 8,000 houses with all the repair and maintenance problems that entails, on top of waiting lists, transfer lists, exchange request, noisy neighbour problems and emergency housing the homeless; landlord for 1,000 or so commercial premises, mostly shops (bringing a number of legal problems), the recreational facilities, three swimming pools, tennis courts, bowling greens, golf courses, pitches of all types and accompanying changing rooms? Fishing rights... you name it they had to administer it according to laws and by-laws and to the public's satisfaction.

Add environment, conservation, planning (from dropped kerbs to multimillion-pound developments), roads, footpaths, pavements and accompanying drains (hundreds of miles of drains) and you can see why the council's turnover adds up to multimillions of pounds per year, with added capital expenditure plus ongoing debts to be serviced.

However, all this can be tripled and quadrupled for County Councillors' responsibilities and most County Councillors will have to travel considerable distances to their Council Chamber and site meetings or to visit constituents because their 'patch' is that much bigger too. No wonder their meetings are held during the daytime. Yet the public would deny them their Attendance Money or Loss of Earnings Allowance for actual Council Meetings (a Councillor can only claim one or the other), still less pay them for expertise or disruption to their family life while attending to all the other related duties.

Attempting to prove I was worth my salt got me a lot of press coverage, not all of it favourable. Fortunately my 'fan club' came to my aid on more that one occasion.

The press items also illustrated my wife's direct involvement. At the very least she had her evenings continually interrupted by telephone calls as constituents attempted to find me at home. Some hope! But where was I when my actual Council meetings averaged only slightly less than one per week? Hence my attendance money was kept so low.

I was out representing the Council on Outside Bodies, necessary Party or Group meetings, related activities such as speaker or in attendance at Action Group meetings of one sort or another; plus my original youth club and allotment committee work and commitments; plus numerous house calls following up my constituents complaints; plus manning Surgeries. On top of this I was an active AUEW union member and some of the work problems can spill over into evening union meetings (AUEW was not then factory-based Branches). Such commitments frequently necessitated attending two meetings per night – sometimes just catching the tail end of a third in an attempt to avoid criticism for non-attendance.

With this workload on top of full-time employment a Councillor certainly needs a back-up home service by a spouse, and by a spouse who can take some knocks. On top of such unsolicited back-up work a spouse is left with no company at home, answering the phone more than five times per evening, being press-ganged into Party, Branch or Constituency business and functions (my wife was not a Party member) typing up long studies, reports and letters and various notices plus attending various functions as the 'Councillor's wife'. Outside Bodies/schools/youth clubs/OAPs functions would feel insulted by anything less.

My wife took it very hard when I was not reselected to stand. My doldrums at the time did nothing to cheer her up either. She received not one word of thanks from the Party even. Small chance that the public would notice her efforts over a seven-year period.

I repeat, a District Councillor's position is no longer a 'do-gooder's' job. It can break up marriages and split families. Financial allowance can never compensate for such treatment for years of work for the electorate generally before you consider direct involvement in Branch activities

– the Councillors' supporting body. My wife laid on much-needed fund-raising activities (but I always paid my full share of election expenses – win or lose) for Branch funds, for example house barbecues, Christmas parties and she helped with car rallies, jumble sales, autumn and spring fairs, etc.

Yet I still understate the family and home involvement.

As with any other manual worker, keeping a home together and bringing up children in a suburban area, a car is essential. However, with mortgage, school extras (piano or French lessons, etc.), normal family holidays expected, not to mention normal household expenses, our finances were stretched even with a working wife. A car, therefore, could only be a 'goer' but no more, i.e. in the old banger class. We had only (up to the end of my Council period) three such cars over a twenty-four-year period but they needed a hell of a lot of attention, visits to scrapyards for bits (whole engines on three occasions) and glass fibre filling and painting. In total they cost only £1,300 to buy, but time fitting exhausts, filling in and respraying wings, (fitting exhaust), replacing points, plugs, leads (fitting exhaust), resetting tappets, plugs, points (fitting exhaust), fitting new distributor cap, resetting plugs, points (fitting exhaust), fitting replacement head, resetting tappets, timing, points, plugs (fitting exhaust), and so on infinitum, around and around, year in year out – including three complete replacement engines built up from the block (short engines). Now this is normal – plus continual starter and/or battery problems – for any manual working family man, but add District Council duties (plus all that entails), and the pressure is on at weekends, even without allotmenting and its Secretary/Treasurer duties, and decorating duties.

My wife had to answer the phone even when I was at home but blacked up to the eyebrows in the garage, or down the allotment.

Add, as we did, house buying and renovating (starting with a new bathroom) and there is no way the telephone is ever going to be answered except by the lady of the house, whatever the hour. I did my renovating and decorating into the early hours of the morning – when else?

And yet that is not all. A few (very few fortunately) constituents find their way to your house at weekends despite all the Surgeries laid on in the Ward. Many more ring up or call during the week but then the house was empty except for the odd day off. On those occasions calls from constituents, press and agencies pegged you down all day. Some day off! These same agencies then sent representatives to discuss a case you had highlighted to them, and keen Welfare Officers or what-have-you would sometimes call at weekends, having failed to make contact for two or three weeks by daytime phone calls. (They could never understand that, always accusing me of being on holiday. Yet they worked in the daytime away from home – why not a Councillor and his wife?)

Thus it was that the local Policeman (when Community Policing started – such were the problems) called on Sunday afternoons. He lived just around the corner, I might add, and came to the monthly Indoor Surgeries from time to time anyway. I was pleased to discuss issues – litter points; hooliganism; dangerous road conditions and junctions; continual complaints of children on roofs, in blocks of flats, back alleys, of gangs in streets; damage to cars parked and so forth. His Sunday calls were genuine reports back or wider in-depth discussions (even though he was scared of my chickens!), and were frequently to tell me he could not do anything. If he saw a light in the garage he would call up to twelve o'clock at night sometimes. Such 'village' coppers do still exist, believe it or not.

One Sunday afternoon I was repairing the family banger on the front drive. I was dressed in oily clothes complete with equally oily woolly hat, the only thing that stays on when under a car, when a very smart Police car pulled up. Out got a very smart peak-capped Police Inspector of over six-foot proportions and an equally well dressed, but petite, lady Constable. They were an engaging pair with very intent faces. I am five-foot two and never dress city gent fashion – I had to buy a suit to wear to the first Mayor-making ceremony! Therefore I do not suppose I exactly looked the Councillor part that day, especially since I was lying partly under the jacked-up car.

Passing me on the way to my 'posh' front door they asked, 'Is Councillor Griffiths in?' somewhat abruptly, without slowing down.

When I replied that I was him, they answered unbelievably, '*The* Councillor Griffiths?' – half stepping towards the front door still not really believing me. No one ever believed I was *the* Councillor Griffiths – the image they had from the press reports was of a pinstriped businessman at least six foot tall and hefty with it.

'Yes. I wrote a memo to you last week regarding a certain troublesome tenant in...'

That seemed to check them somewhat, but they still looked at the front door and back at me under the car a few more times, no doubt expecting the big welcome. But I never had time for such niceties and continued 'mechanicking', it being essential to me to get the car running again ready for a 7 a.m. start the next day and the fitting of yet another scrapyard exhaust had to be completed. With all manual workers, Councillors or otherwise, it's the sack if we miss that 7.30 a.m. clock-in too often. In my case, just once would have been enough (see next chapter). Thus I stayed under the car, oily clothes, woolly hat and all.

Now with my identity established, the Inspector went straight into, 'She is your problem! As a Councillor, get rid of her! Get rid of her within the week!' No further explanation. He then started 'farming' about three inches of my drive by moving his foot to and fro. The lady Constable alternated intent looks at his face then down at me. He kept his eyes on his three-inch farming activity.

Looking out from under the car from time to time I tried to explain, slowly and quietly because of his belligerent mood, that no one Councillor or Council Officer could do that. If anyone had that sort of authority, I would have started the Revolution long ago to get such dictatorial authority off them. In any event, scratching a living on the factory floor all day did not leave me much time to sort such things out – hence Officers were employed and Committees set up to do just that, but it would take time. Meanwhile, should he not enforce law and order particularly where this young tenant and her illegal activities were concerned?

In between some sections of this résumé, he repeated the words, each time more forcefully – 'Get rid of her! Get rid of her within the week!' – and continued, farming my drive. The young lady Constable's eyes were popping out, as if she had very recently seen a ghost or heard a horror story – or both, i.e. the horror story house call followed by me, the ghost of the Councillor she had expected to find.

Clearly they had called to interview the tenant and had not got over the shock. He was 'solving' it by handing it back to me, but was now annoyed to find a working-class git, who had handed it to him in the first place. No big welcome, no sherry in the lounge, and now a debate to boot – I bet he wished he had brought his truncheon with him.

I started quietly outlining what I thought I was paying rates for, from the safety of the underside of the car, including a Police force to sort out the lawbreaking people whether council tenants or otherwise. The happenings I had outlined to him clearly in my memo were offences way past housing problems, although a petition from her neighbours had highlighted the situation initially. Subsequent calls to these neighbours and chats at work to workmates in the immediate area had scared me to death. Plus, the Community Policeman had given me the Inspector's name to contact because the local lad did not want to get involved 'in CID work' as he saw it. (I did not tell the Inspector this last bit, of course.)

By now my concentration in mechanicking had been well and truly broken and I had stood up, resting my aching arms and shoulders by leaning on the car. At 5' 2" and bent over exhausted, I posed no threat to him – I suppose – because his attitude changed.

He said quietly, with no nervous foot movement and leaning his head to about one foot from me, 'If I was to bring charges against all the under-aged lads involved with this single-parent eighteen-year-old girl, and for all the sexual lawbreaking activities they are getting up to in that house after school – all of which she readily outlines, thinking it great fun – then no one, but no one, would believe me. Magistrates could not possibly convict because of the number of under-aged lads involved. Parents would be convinced I had made it all up – the girl would deny everything when advised in court – and the Police would be ostracised on the whole estate for at least two generations. Get rid of her, please, and quick.' He spoke quietly, no bitterness, no hesitation. The Police girl's eyes were still popping out of her head and she was still speechless, whether from fright or the unauthorised solution, I know not.

I did not make any attempt to answer. They paused but briefly, eyes fixed on me, their future in the force in my hands – then left without saying another word. If I did nothing and things got worse, and if I subsequently reported that they had known and done nothing – that would have needed some explaining by them if a parent had taken action.

It took two weeks to solve it via a chat or two to workmates who lived in her original village. The Inspector probably spent the time job hunting! It was solved via the Housing Officer by getting her mother to exchange houses. Back in her village the local lads (married men) several of whom thought they were the father of her two children, 'protected' her from outsiders, including schoolboys who cycled over. The local lads wanted her for themselves, of course, as per the norm before she was housed. Thus they kept the peace, as it were.

I never heard another word from anyone except a nod across the Council Chamber from the Housing Officer the day of the house exchange just two weeks later. We were relieved! To speak by any other means than a nod would have been disastrous because transfers were in great demand. There were long waiting lists, and they should have been granted, if at all, via Committees where troublesome tenants were concerned. But time was not on anyone's side – least of all our nervous six-foot-odd Police Inspector's – and the cat would have been out of the bag if taken through Committee.

However, I tell the story now to show that a Councillor's Sunday afternoons are not quite as peaceful as most other people's.

I have a memo story of another pleasant sunny Sunday afternoon spent with a tenant and a Policeman. I was answering a call from a Council Home Warden on that occasion. Council Officers do not allow their private telephone numbers or their addresses into general circulation, not even to their Wardens. It's easy to see why – they would never get a Sunday in peace if they did.

Meanwhile, with such worries to solve, I had to get the car running to catch that 7.30 a.m. factory clock, thereafter to be hounded by Supervisors all day who were intent on proving I was a useless Socialist who they were going to sort out. They were determined to strike a blow for Company and Country by turning back the onslaught of 'Socialist Doctrine'. Just what do such phrases as 'Socialist Doctrine' mean when all you are trying to do is sort out other people's problems and ensure the District Council systems work effectively to the good of one and all – including Supervisors?

The next chapter will give the story – judge for yourselves.

Time-off-work Problems

I do not wish to give the impression that problems getting time off work were peculiar to me or to my employer. The then *Labour Weekly* did from time to time give examples of newly appointed Magistrates being told bluntly by their small-firm employers, 'Refuse the appointment or pack your job in.' I suspect many, many more people employed in small firms just do not attempt any public duties knowing full well it would sooner or later cause a clash with their employer. Thus the problem is, overtly or covertly, general.

Workers have a basic and fundamental duty to their families, therefore such clashes with their employers, for whatever reason, have to be avoided if at all possible. It is possible to keep out of public office, and this they do to avoid conflict of interests antagonising their employer and thereby putting promotion or their job at risk.

This last point was a common enough one put to me by workmates; therefore it must be held by many, if not most, members of the public. My employer, or more precisely the Company's junior managers who were over me, were such members of the public. Furthermore, they had the problem of finding someone to do my job while I was off work, attending to electors' business – albeit unpaid.

It so happened (it would!) that my particular work situation left my Supervisors little room for manoeuvre even if we ignore the Senior Managers on their backs. I was a skilled First Off Inspector in a busy Machine Shop Section of 155 machines, forty-five operators and sixteen setters, with work encompassing drilling, broaching, turning, presses and heat-hardening processes. More than 30,000 components per day passed through from raw casting stage to finished condition. There was only one First Off Inspector per Section. To arrange cover for me only left another Section short-handed. Any absence left a hole and a headache for Supervision even in a large multinational firm, which employed 7,000-plus on the local site. It must leave even greater gaps in a small firm with perhaps only four or five employees.

Turning down overtime to attend duties was frowned upon. Most skilled men are expected to maintain regular and consistent overtime including Sundays, if only to ensure a full start on Monday mornings, meaning machines repaired, set up and passed off, assembly tracks changed over and the first batch of five passed off, and so forth ready for Monday mornings.

Thus Management wanted me at work, yet Council duties inevitably meant some daytime duties during working hours.

It was a dilemma! I wanted time off to carry out Council duties in line with my democratic rights on behalf of my constituents, indeed as I signed to do when sworn in as a Councillor. Managers or employers wanted me at work in accordance with my forty hours (thirty-nine now) Contract of Employment as I signed to do when entering their service (conveniently forgotten during short time periods?).

This problem had been solved satisfactorily and all had worked well before the days of foreign competition in the Car Industry. The Personnel Department had agreed that employees with public duties to perform should have time off, plus make-up pay, so long as it was 'not excessive'. In practice that had been as much as two days per week for employees who were County Councillors and Magistrates but these were usually staff employees. I only ever attempted to get five or six days per year, spread over ten or twelve part days. I did not think this was excessive. It was less than many employees took without permission with no questions ever asked. They were just absent for a half day or two along the way. I applied in writing well in advance in order to help administration, yet still got into trouble despite the Personnel Officer repeatedly assuring me all would be well so long as I gave local management advance notice in writing. He supplied me with a Company memo pad to do just that, in fact.

None of these arrangements cut any ice with my immediate Supervisors who either did not know of them or did not wish to accommodate them or just wished to obstruct things, or a combination of all three possibilities. Supervisors changed so frequently that it was seldom possible to form an opinion. I was deep in trouble with a three-day suspension under my belt before I realised that leaving work to perform Council or Council-related duties was a serious problem not easily resolved. Naively I thought that in a democracy a mouse may look at a queen and everyone had a democratic right to carry out elected duties. Black men in South Africa know differently, of course, but I was yet to learn that I was the black man in Britain – a point I was to make in the press before being released from the battle by non-selection by my Labour Branch some years down the line.

My three-day suspension (reduced from dismissal, to five days then to three days) was for leaving the factory without a Pass Out. I had a Christmas School Governors' 'thank you' function to attend – picking up my wife en route. Refused a Pass Out and not wishing to risk a divorce by leaving my wife at the roadside outside her place of employment in 8 December weather, I left – clocking out, of course. No payment was asked for or expected from any quarter. I was just carrying out a duty on behalf of my constituents. But leaving work without a pass, or moving from one Division to another inside the factory, e.g. to Pay Office or Personnel Department, is a diabolical crime. The Personnel Officer opened the proceedings with the words 'The charge is...', never a simple 'Can we clear up this misunderstanding?' or 'There appears to be a problem...'

Then a succession of disciplinary actions curbed my democratic rights considerably and on the few occasions I did get a pass it was usually only after heated debates leaving me in no mood to sit through Selection Meetings, school disciplinary sessions, or even to concentrate on Council Agenda matters, still less chair five hours of Warwickshire Protection Council meetings with top officers from four Districts, plus intent fellow Councillors present from four Districts. (Manual workers had no 'discretionary' days off to use up for such occasions.)

As the press items indicated, the alternative is to leave democracy in the hands of OAPs, the unemployed and the upper classes.

The mass of the population, i.e. the working population (the actual PAYE tax payers) go under- or unrepresented. America fought a war of Independence over the point. We, the workers, either cannot hold public office or, when holding public office, fall down in our duties, being unable to attend to them fully. Public offices are closed during our free hours, likewise all other agencies a Councillor needs to contact from time to time to argue a constituent's case or to check on what his employees (public servants) are doing. On top of this, site meetings, inspections and interviews are frequently only possible in normal working daytime hours because:

a) during winter sites are in the dark outside working hours (for about four months of the year a manual worker goes to work and travels home in the dark);

b) the particular problem needing attention only occurs under daytime working conditions, e.g. excessive traffic, noise, heavy lorries, obstruction, dangerous road conditions, junctions, buses turning dangerously outside school gates;

c) other agencies only work normal hours, e.g. road repair gangs, refuse collectors, welfare workers for case studies, as well as the office hours problem above and;

d) people travelling to selection interviews, e.g. teachers or youth workers, may be coming some distance and have family commitments to get back to even if the journey times allow evening interviews, and they are willing to attend at such odd hours even if Officers are prepared to forfeit yet another evening to attend during out-of-office hours.

I might add that it is not only Shop Stewards or Council staff who do not expect to meet their employers (Councillors) in the evenings for regular (normal) management meetings. Teachers' Union reps and full-time professional youth leaders do not expect to carry out managerial meetings in the evenings either nowadays. And why should they? You wouldn't.

Thus from time to time, depending on a Councillor's amount of involvement (though some Councillor must do it even if another drops it) a Councillor will need time off work to attend to Council or Council-related duties during the day.

The public are split on this issue just as they are over Attendance Money payments for council meetings. Just how an institution with over 900 employees (more than 33,000 at county level) can be run by a few do-gooders spending a few hours now and again in the evenings, I do not know. I used to ask my Supervisors, 'Why don't you take a shop-floor job and come back and manage the Company [their bit of it] in your spare time in the evenings?' The question never made any impression mainly because they in no way saw the need for any 'managing' of a Council. They were in the 'I can do my own councilloring' group, hence the sermon I heard often enough to know it off by heart. 'If no one is absent, off sick, wants to go racing, sail a model boat or fly a model aeroplane, then I can release you,' clearly indicating that attending to District Council duties was less essential than any of these activities. No wonder they maintained they could do their own councilloring. It would be nice to be so ignorant.

Fellow Councillors will quickly realise why such a discussion just to get a Pass Out from work quickly elevated into a shouting match. I would retort in equally memorised words, 'You cannot even buy a packet of soap powder without the aid of a Councillor from the moment you leave your house to returning to it – the road you drive along has been straightened, surfaced, white-lined, yellow-lined, kerbed by decisions of Councillors. The signs indicating the way into town, the direction to the public car park, shopping centre, the layout, landscaping, surfacing, charges and method of collecting car park charges, have all been decided by Councillors: pulling the houses down to make room for the car park was a Councillor's decision, where replacement estates were built, services and amenities on those estates were Councillors' decisions, attending to the resulting problems caused by such movements of people and communities just to accommodate your car has to be done by Councillors. Which shops sell what and the balance of shops to offices were Councillors' decisions. Even the level of music played while you buy your soap powder would have to be controlled by the Councillors sitting on an

Environmental Committee if complaints were made about it. The type of window, maintenance of the shop front, the size and type of shop signs, even the colour of the outside paintwork in Leamington's Conservation area are all decided by Councillors. These things all in turn affect the price you pay for your soap powder and the level of your rates. The air you breathe throughout the journey is kept reasonably clean by Councillors' decisions – especially mine on both Warwickshire and District Environmental Committees. Now how the hell do you do your own councilloring?'

The rest of such discussions would not make suitable reading for delicate readers, but even the résumé was an understatement – their house designs, position of their house, even the colour of bricks, roof and tiles were all decided on by Councillors, just as the gas, electricity, sewage and drain services were all similarly decided on. Of course, the money for most of these services, especially those in the first résumé, has to be raised, collected, borrowed and repaid – all Councillors' decisions with the threat of surcharge if mistakes are made at any stage.

It's a lot easier to pretend you can do your own councilloring!

There were some funny twists as time went on. For example it took a two-hour argument to get a Pass Out from a Foreman to go to a Special Governors' meeting to discuss a parents' petition complaining about the Head's methods. Arriving breathless after the meeting had started I asked for the petition to check its authority: how many, if any, had signed twice? Were the numbers representing one per household or were whole families signing individually, inflating the figure? Did signatures come from parents within the school's catchment area? (Anyone can stand on the main shopping street and get pages of signatures for whatever cause!) This is the sort of thing, like looking through applicants' forms before interviewing, that it would be nice to arrive in time to do before such meetings. Big arguments at work and a last-minute Pass was no help even when I did get a Pass Out.

This petition was genuine, but halfway down the second page there was the signature of the very Foreman who had been arguing, 'You owe the Company forty hours.' He had petitioned the Governors to do something for his children – but in the Governor's own time, of course! And why should a Head and Deputy come back in their own time to sort out working methods? That same Foreman would soon have his union rep on the job if he was expected to do that for his employer.

That same Foreman refused a Pass Out for me to attend an Appeal Tribunal on behalf of a workmate who was also a constituent (as many were) and whom I had arranged to meet in the Works' car park in order to travel together. Only when the workmate returned to the Section gesticulating, indicating we were out of time for the Hearing, did I get a Pass Out. We won the appeal – which was called hours after the stated time in the normal fashion – but it would have been lost by default with a stigma against his name for life, but for the chance that he could come back into the factory and help me apply pressure on the Foreman.

Normal Management Union channels did not solve these situations. That took days, or even weeks. The Personnel Department always agreed I could get Passes, but actually obtaining one in time to leave remained the difficulty.

But the same Personnel Department also added their own twist. Sooner or later in any upgrading or promotion interviews the questioning stuck on, 'You are very involved with outside activities. If you were asked to be a Magistrate, would you accept? Because we do not want a part-timer?' End of interview and no upgrading or promotion. Seventeen qualifications including an Open University Degree counted for nothing unless I gave up the outside activities. Who was running the Factory? The local Masonry Lodge in my opinion.

On one such occasion the only question asked by the chief personnel officer was, 'If you get this job, will you promise me you will give up all your outside activities?'

'No.'

'You are wasting my time,' he blasted out, spreading his arms wide in the air in utter frustration. End of interview (that was the complete interview in fact). Another £2,000 per year down the drain, and I never applied for any more jobs internally – that was the thirteenth try, in fact. Such interviews undermine your morale and confidence. It's easier to live without such knocks from time to time, especially when you know you are not going to get the job anyway.

That Personnel Officer was a constituent of mine, quite favourably disposed towards me – hence the shortlist interview in the first place. Six months earlier his signature was the second (the first one was a Foreman's) on a petition from his whole street begging me to get rid of a particularly noisy and ill-behaved council-house neighbour just across the street from him. This was the eighteen-year-old tenant in the previous chapter, in fact, who had the Police Inspector wrong-footed as well.

Just who would attend to such problems if we all took his advice and gave up outside activities in order to get promotion, another £2,000 a year and a company car?

Of course, his noisy neighbour has long since gone. I arranged a house swap with her mother within a couple of weeks – the Police also calling at my house to get me to do something, 'otherwise half the youth on the estate would have to be arrested and the backlash effect would sour relations with the Police for the next two generations'.

However, I was annually still £2,000 down and still drove and maintained old banger cars. To compensate my low earnings my wife still worked however much her arthritis played up. Meanwhile the ex-Chief Personnel Officer relaxed at home in quiet and peaceful surroundings enjoying a fat company pension.

Life can be cruel – ask my wife.

Knocks from immediate Supervisors at work came often and hard. When first elected, my Superintendent of that time 'congratulated' me with the words, 'Labour could put a monkey up in that Ward and win.'

It had been first won for Labour four years earlier and Labour lost it decisively when I was not reselected, seven years later. Such comments come very hard. Why say anything if that is what they really think – or were they jealous?

Despite arrangements – standard for all Councillors with the firm – with the Personnel Officer, another request for a Pass Out to attend a School function was blandly refused with the words, 'You don't get passes to ass about down the town.' This was a year after my being suspended for three days for leaving without a Pass Out to attend the same annual function, and I had yet again received reassurances at Personnel level that Passes would be issued. I carefully explained that my children had left school; I was now attending to school duties on behalf of the electorate. Further I had made arrangements to pick my wife up outside her place of employment since she had also been invited in her capacity of Governor's wife.

'I don't care what you prats get up to, you are not getting a Pass Out,' was the insulting reply snapped back by the Foreman as he turned and walked away – a different Foreman from the previous occasions.

I caught him up in just five steps, and barring his way, I asked slowly and carefully, 'Would you care to rephrase that last remark or apologise?'

He brushed me aside with his hand and walked briskly past me stating, 'I don't have to apologise to idiots like you.'

I was in front of him again in less than two steps this time and said very firmly with no intention of being brushed aside, 'Would you accompany me to the Personnel Office, please?'

His eyes wandered over my head and his body went limp as he found himself at a loss. He slowly turned back to my bench – myself 'guarding' him from behind in case he tried to bolt again. He took his Pass Book out of his pocket and filled it in without a murmur, but as he handed the Pass Out to me and slipped past me leaving, he said, 'I still say you are only going pissing about down town.'

Such interludes put you in an excellent frame of mind to commence Christmas School Governor duties – I don't think! Yet a hasty word, sharp reply, faulty decision by me at the function resulting from such frustrating situations just before the engagement and I would be regarded as a very odd Councillor and Governor. I personally thought the Supervisors the odd ones – but others see it differently, as letters to the press confirmed. But do the public know they are undermining democracy by encouraging such odd behaviour by Supervisors?

I would spend twenty or even thirty minutes looking for my Foreman just before requiring a Pass Out, my initial request having been submitted in writing up to two weeks earlier in line with arrangements with Personnel Office. In desperation I would start asking other Foremen. They would always ask, 'Have you asked your Foreman?' 'Couldn't find him,' was no excuse – they always explained it was up to him to issue the Pass because they did not know if he had arranged cover for me on the Section. A valid point, but no help to me with a meeting deadline slipping past. Council meetings, School Governor meetings, Youth Centre Selection meetings (I was Chairman) just do not start at any old time – they start pronto in accordance with Notice of Meeting. Besides, is it fair to keep staff, parents and Education Officers waiting? They all have jobs too.

On one occasion a Production Foreman (and Party member) did issue me with a Pass Out. As I left the building my Foreman appeared out of the blue and chased me all the way down to the Police Gate, threatening to discipline me if I insisted on leaving, Pass or no Pass. No Foreman, friendly or otherwise, dared risk issuing me with a Pass Out after that episode. They had their promotion to think of too.

The pressures that built up due to the hounding I took at work both because of the few requests for time off and from the straightforward mickey taking in an 'I'll-put-him-in-his-place' approach were by far the worst problems I faced during the whole seven years I held office. It evaporated over night when I lost office, needless to say.

Perhaps you are thinking that ten or twelve battles per year to get a Pass Out from work is not much to worry about. It did not stop there!

Photostat copies of press reports of my comments in Council were thrust under my nose and explanations demanded, followed by lectures about 'loyalty'. 'Loyalty' presumably meant I should take a non-Socialist stance in Council irrespective of how my electorate voted.

With written warnings and a three-day Suspension behind me I was on a tightrope, of course. The sack is the only other step in discipline procedure. When a day of action was called by the AUEW, the local Shop Stewards decided on a walkout and march to a rally in town. I dared not join such a walkout. While the rest would get (and did get) a warning, I would get the sack. Against this, I dared not stay in because of the ridicule a known activist would get for not joining officially requested union action.

I solved the problem by being absent (a very rare thing

for me) for the whole day and joining the rally in town. I did not think the men would march from the factory gates to the rally – but they did!

Back at work the next morning I was immediately approached by the Foreman to explain my absence. Scores of men were absent any and every day, including on that day, but I was the only one approached to explain my one-day absence. My only reply was that I was 'absent'.

After about twenty minutes of trying to prise a further answer out of me on that point the Foreman then repeatedly asked if I was on the march (all Foremen made such lists on that point). I refused to answer, arguing that what I chose to do on a day off was my own affair and nothing to do with my employer. After thirty minutes or more persistent pressing the Foreman, clearly under instructions, announced he was putting me on the list of those on the march (which was incorrect) and left.

You cannot win however you play it, but I did avoid the sack.

The continual hounding got so bad under another Foreman – they change very frequently – that I eventually accepted a Shop Steward's support and brought a victimisation charge against him on eight counts. Men were willing to give evidence against the Foreman by then because even they had got sickened with it – as had some of the Foremen and Supervisors themselves. I must clearly state here that the vast majority of Foremen and Supervisors were always kindly disposed towards me. You do not work twenty-one years in a place (as I had up to then) and not fit in. Besides, many had sought my advice or sent workers to me for advice. Also I had been moved several times on to Sections to replace men cracking up under the strain – literally. Indeed, this particular Foreman had requested me because he had heard I was 'the only man capable of sorting out' his big Section. Such a posting made any absence even more critical, of course. Thus the time soon came when that same Foreman had to be stopped before he manipulated me down the road for good – big Section or otherwise.

Thus I listed the eight points of victimisation as follows:

1. Despite arrangements whereby I give ten to fourteen days prior written notice, the Foreman dodges the time just when I need a Pass Out by 'hiding' in another Division.

2. After the very few occasions I am out, I have to wait in his Office to see if I have a job to return to – no other employee has to do this.

3. I was not allowed Foreman level, Superintendent level or local Shop Steward representations when disciplined for these imaginary crimes, but sent straight to Personnel for 'sanctioning'.

4. False information given in these disciplinary 'charges'.

5. Object strongly to the phrase 'All you do-gooders need locking up' as stated by the Foreman.

6. I'm hounded on the shop floor by the Foreman over every press item about me as a Councillor.

7. Hounded continually about potholes in the roads here, there and everywhere but I'm refused a Pass Out to follow up the Foreman's pothole complaints.

8. Continually hounded about any aspect of life which annoys the Foreman, e.g. young people in wheelchairs 'playing' outside his house; how football fans should be beaten up by Police to stop their singing; patients should not be allowed into town from the local psychiatric hospital.

I added that I now considered I had been 'set up' by him when he asked for me to move on to his big Section because I was both capable of controlling the Section and keeping an eye on a trainee already on the area. I now found the trainee got preference – except on his school day when I got the lot. I might add I also objected to having to state in detail where I was going, to which Committees, and for what purpose I needed to attend them – thereupon to be given a lecture on what I should say before being refused a Pass Out. I got the feeling I would have no trouble if I indicated I would follow his extreme Right Wing line of argument.

My Steward took the list to the Manager. It appeared pointless to go through Foreman level, and anyway I had not been afforded Foreman level, just whipped up to the Personnel Office and 'charged', with no lower level allowed. They jumped local Shop Steward's representation as well in the process.

The Manager told my Steward it must come through Foreman level first – a sudden return to correct procedures! At Foreman level – the very same Foreman, of course – he asked for specific examples. I took out a newspaper cutting about a trainee Probation Officer (a Bank Manager's son) who had been given three months' sentence for rioting at a football match. I handed it in to the Shop Steward, then the witnessing Foreman, and then asked my trouble-making Foreman if he accepted that he gave me the cutting with the statement, 'That's you do-gooders – you all want locking up.'

He readily agreed he had and went straight into an often repeated citation about the country never getting on its feet until the Welfare State had been dismantled, and so forth and so on – the witnessing Foreman showing an interest in proceedings for the first time at this.

That general line of putting the country on its feet by defeating Socialism and dismantling the Welfare State was gone over by him several times in between stating, point by point, that there was no charge to answer.

'Case thrown out.' No 'Failure to agree' registered, no further stage allowed – 'Problem solved' was his winding up.

Even the witnessing Foreman thought a 'Failure to Agree' could and should be registered since we clearly did not accept his line of argument on any point – those connected with the issues or his anti-Socialist yamperings.

Back went the Shop Steward to the Manager. He took two weeks to reply – then he said he would accept 'Failure to agree' if a more senior witnessing Foreman was present at Foreman stage and thought it appropriate. (There had been no such time delays or toing and froing at Foreman level when I had been charged.) This done, the Manager said it could and should be sorted out at Foreman level. Thus, two more Forman-level meetings followed – one with yet another witnessing Foreman who agreed 'Failure to agree' should be registered and the serious issues resolved at Personnel level. The Manager then refused to allow any more discussion on the subject and did not indicate if any problem existed or otherwise.

It would be nice if workers could get out of tricky situations so neatly. I had never been allowed even a Foreman-level discussion when I had been 'charged'. Indeed to this day I have yet to be taken into a Foreman's office and told I cannot have a Pass Out. The problem always was that they refused to give me one when requested despite one or even two weeks' advanced warning. The only purpose served by an advanced request was that they could 'hide' by being 'busy' in another division at the time a Pass Out was needed.

This whole unsatisfactory situation at work can make a busy man very, very demoralised – as it was planned to do. People who think democracy is working might ponder the point that it only works for those who are allowed to partake. For the vast majority of workers, it is a sham. Most do not even try to operate it, knowing the difficulties are insurmountable.

By this time I had failed reselection for the Ward – at least some of those selecting taking the view that to continue would cost me my job. And 'some' out of the selection Committee of eight left me one short of reselection. Democracy took yet another knock.

From that time until my term as a councillor finished I reverted to normal practice when requesting a Pass Out: I ignored arrangements whereby I informed Management well in advance. I now did like any other employee. I went into the Foreman's Office and asked for a Pass Out about ten minutes before leaving, only stating 'Appointment'. It was only two or three occasions anyway in that five-month period – as was the norm. I just repeated 'Appointment' whatever subsequent questions were put to me. I had long since abandoned requesting make-up pay, the amount being not worth the hassle. By my stating 'Appointment' the Foreman must either refuse the majority who also stated 'Appointment' or leave himself open to yet another victimisation merry-go-round.

Of Clerks, Cabbages and Cockerels

Some things happened to me, or there are things I did, during my period of office, which do not fit into any category but, nevertheless, are worthy of a mention in this short résumé of a Councillor's activities. Other Councillors get involved in similar issues, some more so than myself because they are of different ethnic backgrounds or may have Welfare-type jobs and are more accessible than even I tried to make myself. It would be unfair to them not to mention these other issues here.

The first might be a little doubtful as to its Councillor nature unless you are non-English or you are a black or Asian Councillor. It happens to them in all walks of life, unfortunately.

The very first mailing of District Council papers included an application form to join the League of St George. Hardly a District Council paper, so why was it included?

In the Midlands, I have always been regarded as a Welshman. The press frequently referred to me as Welsh-born. With Griffiths as a surname and a strong Welsh-border accent it is difficult to suggest otherwise. Since everyone calls me 'Hughie' I have long since signed myself as such – but it is not my real forename (the shop floor would not accept Humphrey!). In fact I am English, born just one and a half miles inside Herefordshire on the Monmouthshire border – a whole county away from Wales at the time but now only one and a half miles away because Monmouthshire 'drifted' back to Wales due to some pussyfooting by England during the 1939–45 war. I arrived in the Midlands, actually in Leamington itself, in 1949 when I was just eighteen. I served five and a half years in Warwickshire battalions to boot, but I have a Welsh name and a Welsh-border accent, therefore I must be Welsh according to Midlanders. English, Welsh, Pakistani – does it matter? We all have to live somewhere and we are all human beings working to keep house and home together.

Well it mattered to one District Council Officer, because the League of St George application form slipped in with the very first papers clearly said, 'Go home.'

Leamington (Priors) was a village of only 300 people in the 1811 census. It boomed in Klondike gold rush fashion in the first half of that century when 'taking the waters' was fashionable. It has continued growing ever since and it is still growing. Very few people living in Leamington are true Leamingtonians of more than five generations or so. I wonder where that particular Officer's grandparents, or parents even, came from?

I pondered for a long time what to do about the St George's League form, even keeping it for a year or more, but decided to let it ride when no follow-up occurred.

I guess black and Asian Councillors come off much, much worse, and getting time off work must be impossible for them as well.

Back to duties and a much more pleasant aspect of a Councillor's work.

Even before being elected a District Councillor, I had frequently been approached at work by workmates needing advice on family, household or school matters – it's part of any Shop Steward's day. Occasionally it would transpire that their real problem was drafting a letter that would scan in a middle-class-style phraseology and thus stand a better chance of getting the required result. These inquirers were not ignorant; some were immigrants from the Indian Subcontinent and spoke and often wrote three languages.

Others were workers not practised in letter writing, but all were intelligent and knew the advantages of a nicely worded letter laid out in request form – not demands – making a point firmly without appearing to threaten; an opening statement, respectful ending, yet short and to the point type of letter. These might be letters to Income Tax Inspectors, Immigrant Officials, Gas Board, Electricity Board, hire purchase firms as well as to Council offices. Letters to School Heads were always a regular and still are.

This letter-drafting continued and grew apace during my term in office. However, as the Indian immigrant population increased they turned to their own letter-writers – a profession in their culture.

Once the 'give away' reductions of up to 50% to tenants buying their council houses started, advice on house purchasing was required – approximate repayments on a mortgage for comparison with current rent. I rapidly realised it was necessary to cover the subject more deeply, including researching how to shop around for mortgages, otherwise tenants automatically accepted a Council mortgage not realising they were free to negotiate one anywhere, especially with upwards of half a house as a deposit. Once ex-tenants had signed for a Council mortgage it proved impossible to get a mortgage transferred. Building societies and banks had all the new business they could handle without such complications.

This advice on how to negotiate the purchase of their house could stretch into three to six sessions; even then the constituent or workmate would want to check back at each step to keep their confidence up. Buying a house was the biggest thing even a middle-aged man had ever done or was ever likely to do. I had been through it three times and, coming from farming stock, I found purchases less worrying than the handshake deals my father had survived on.

Another sideline of any Councillor is advising

constituents of their rights, e.g. welfare benefits, rate/rent rebates, heating/fuel rebates, school meals, clothes, travel allowances, Special School/training centre possibilities for the handicapped children – the list is endless and always growing. Frequently it boiled down to confirming such possibilities existed and writing down the address to write to for further details. Occasionally such inquiries necessitated quite a lot of checking out – even lost time from work to represent a constituent at an Appeal Tribunal for one reason or another.

Thus it was that I attended several Tribunals assisting Claims for Sick Benefit following DHSS refusal to pay it on the grounds that 'by the law of averages a person could not be off sick three or four times a year, or over Christmas and over Easter' as the case may be. It seemed odd to me that a sick person must decide to be well to suit the Law of Averages, while on the other hand a fit person must decide to be ill from time to time to balance the DHSS view of statistics. Only Civil Servants do the latter, in order to use up their full sick leave entitlement every year. Quite obviously the 'laws' work the other way around where sickness is concerned. Some people never need a Doctor all their lives while others are much less robust from birth and catch everything. Still others, unfortunately, are born with incurable problems such as Down's syndrome and are 'ill' all their lives. Oh, were it so that they could decide to be well to balance the DHSS averages – but who would pick the person to take a turn with Down's Syndrome?

However, young, keen twenty-three- or twenty-four-year-old 'investigation clerks' from the DHSS do not worry about such things. They boldly state at Tribunals that the Law of Averages dictates how often a person can be ill over, say, five-, ten- or fifteen-year periods.

My first such case was a constituent who had been off work 246 times since the conception of the National Health

Service in 1946. Despite Doctor's notes his sick benefit was refused for the second time in a few months and bills were piling up at home.

He had been a Bevin Boy – drafted down the pits – during the 1939–45 war and, like all Bevin Boys, had to stay on two years after the war had finished. He was a hard worker with twenty-seven years of service with his current employer, active in local voluntary work including gala days and sports days and Treasurer of a local Social Club (paying OAPs electric bills and so forth). From his pit days – which he hated and which had played on his nerves – he had suffered with leg ulcers, which broke out into weeping festers from time to time. In between he often had trouble getting a shoe on in the mornings because his foot would swell up for periods prior to the ulcers bursting. As he aged, he looked seventy but was only fifty-one; all sorts of other related ailments were triggered and added to his problems. He had got to the stage of struggling to work for the company between stages of bedridden rest to keep these ailments down. There was no War Pension, or British Legion help for Bevin Boy 'War Wounds' – only young DHSS clerks stating he was not fitting their averages, therefore he must be fit to work.

After I had completed the above résumé, the Tribunal President asked him just one question: 'How many tubes of ointment do you use per month?'

'Three,' said Andy, looking him straight in the eye – but, of course, there were periods when he used none when other ailments laid him up.

He got his sick benefit plus the amount owed for the previous unpaid sick period as well, which we had not challenged thinking it too late to do so!

Doctors do not take up such cases because they argue their signed Sick Notes should suffice. 'It says what it says' – their professional conduct should not be questioned. Also they argue that to get involved in such 'Welfare Work' would distract them from their medical care duties. They have a point. But it leaves their patients in no-man's-land as far as sick payments are concerned when stopped by the DHSS.

I had a succession of such cases following that initial success – which no one thought I would win, assuming incorrectly that I would base my submission on medical evidence. Even the Panel President opened by addressing me sharply with, 'You wish to present further medical evidence on behalf of this man?'

'No,' I said and he whipped his glasses off in stunned amazement. I kept him thus wrong-footed, hence his one and only question at the end. His two fellow panellists never caught up – no one asked Andy for his assessment, which might have let them in on the questioning.

Andy died, aged only fifty-four, while this was being typed.

I won all the Sick Benefit cases and the demand dropped off long before I finished as a Councillor. I like to think the young DHSS statistical clerks got the message. However, I did come unstuck with a different appeal case – in more ways than one!

The initial contact started normally enough, with a telephone call with the caller giving other constituents' names who had recommended me. The trouble was he kept running out of 10ps. I mean really running out, and ringing back several minutes later to repeat himself. After about three shots of this I realised he had no money and was accosting passers-by for 10ps between calls. It was a bitter cold night for such an exercise in survival tactics to boot.

Getting his address I went around to him on a house call immediately to check his problem out. This is an essential process for constituents you do not know, to make sure it is a 'client' who is reasonably presentable and with sufficient resolve to hold firm under questioning by whomever. Lesser mortals need other help. He was about thirty years old, unemployed, a bit run down and dishevelled and of a nervous disposition – not good material but not too bad either, provided I could harness his nerves. Anyway, his story held up under my questioning, and he really needed helping. There were no other agencies he could go to for the assistance he needed, i.e. presenting his case at an Appeal Tribunal which was due two days later.

His single-person council flat was two floors up. Right in the middle of a bitter winter spell his window had been broken by a lump of ice used as a stone – probably aimed at the brickwork. The council's repair policy did not cover broken windows, nor broken toilets, washbasins or baths, unless from genuine wear. This I knew, of course, having long since obtained all relevant documents setting out tenants' rules and procedures. He had, therefore, been forced to get his window repaired at a cost of £35 in order to prevent himself dying of the cold. The charge was reasonable – two floors up, working in bitter weather, replacing a large glass pane over four foot square. It was also just too big a job for a DIY man (which he obviously was not) supposing ladders and tools could be stored in a single-person flat, ready and waiting for such a job of maintenance, which they cannot. He had to pay cash in advance to get anyone to do it at all.

His problem was that he now had no money left to meet gas and electric bills, nor any to buy food with even – hence his predicament in the phone box.

Christ, he lived frugally; walking around town, lingering in shops, libraries, offices, anywhere so long as it was warm, in order to save on fuel bills. His electric bill had been only £4.10 for the previous quarter. He ate sandwich-style meals to avoid using the gas cooker.

The council's repair policy was harsh, aimed at keeping

down wilful damage by tenants in their own homes. It is possible to get fed up with continually replacing windows, toilets, washbasins, even outside doors after family rows or parties. However, his predicament was also harsh and obvious. One big unexpected bill and he was broke. His meagre bread-butter-and-jam food supplies had run out too and he had no workmate-type friends to borrow from. In fact, he had obviously been supplementing a single-parent girl he had just met and was dotty about until – bang! £35 for a window! The girl had got problems enough without his. No help there.

The DHSS would not refund the money, arguing that his small 'Sup-Ben' payment had a built-in amount to cover such contingencies. They sent him to the Council's Housing Department. The Council would not fork out, hiding behind the Committee-approved laid-down policy. They sent him to the Citizens Advice Bureau. The CAB knew of no other channels and sent him back to the DHSS. Round and round these three offices, spread out in town, in bitter cold weather, with no overcoat and only half fed, he had gone.

It was lucky he had sufficient self-esteem left to accost passers-by for only 10ps to ring me with – anyone else would have demanded £10!

By now it was Sunday and his next Giro cheque would not arrive until the following Thursday. With six to eight inches of snow and ice on the ground, it might not arrive even then. With no money for his meters and no food he rang me.

I gave him £1 with instructions to buy only bread to go with bits of sauce he had left in his cupboard (the corner shop was open). I would take his case at the Tribunal Hearing on the following Tuesday. I then spent two hours of my Sunday afternoon laying down strict instructions on what he was to say (only) at the Tribunal, how to present himself, hairstyle, clothes, demeanour – and telling him not to keep rattling on about his new-found single-parent girlfriend (probably his very first girlfriend). The last thing the Tribunal would want to hear was how he 'really wanted to help her'. He thought this was a point in his favour, of course.

I picked him up on the Tuesday morning. He was reasonably presentable – no overcoat, but with the seam burst open on one shoulder of his only jacket. His hair was still shoulder length – I had forgotten hair cuts cost money also, but I fortunately worked it out in time to refrain from comment. I cut my own hair. I should have taken my hair-cutting kit with me on the house call – it was a job I did when on manoeuvres in the Army. His nervousness was inborn, hence he lived in a single-person flat without friends of a lasting nature.

The Hearing was due for 11.30 but by 12.30 we were still waiting. He was still refusing to sit down and relax. On Inquiry, after he had combed his hair for the 500th time, I discovered he had not eaten for twenty-four hours again. Bang went any hope of him giving a favourable performance under questioning. So! Another £1 and a quick trip to a shop fixed him up with biscuits and a Mars bar – the Mars bar for his spirits, the biscuits for his hunger. He had to settle on the men's washroom facilities for liquid refreshment I'm afraid. It is easy to be way out of pocket if you fail to draw the line somewhere.

The Panel would not believe that the District Council would not pay for the window – Coventry's Labour Council, where we now were, apparently did. They spoke very sharply to me as if I were telling lies or it was my fault for allowing such a policy – my Party's three to one minority position having no bearing on the issue apparently. My man kept wanting to open up. I silenced him by the simple means of treading on his foot, and keeping my foot continually pressed hard down, increasing the pressure to pain barrier level every time he attempted to continue 'yes' or 'no' answers. The last thing I wanted to hear in there was the life history of his new-found single-parent girlfriend.

The Panel adjourned and presumably rang for confirmation of the Council's policy, because when they returned they were very sympathetic – but! They explained such emergency bills were taken care of by built-in contingencies in his 'Sup-Ben' allowance. They could not find money for other bills outstanding as a result of him paying this one – conveniently ignoring the fact that he had had to pay in advance to get the job done at all. Had he not paid this one, things might be different owing to his desperate state. However, he had paid it, therefore they could not pay it again, that was their conclusion. They advised back to the Council – said with vague looks on their faces knowing damn well it was valueless advice only added to make it possible for them to sleep at night.

Case lost, and we were ushered out pronto. No time to make a scene.

I dropped him off, giving him another £1 for bread (only) again. He hung on to the car door handle repeating over and over, 'What do I do, what do I do?' I could only answer 'Riot' as I drove off.

I still do not know any better advice; at least rioting is better than mugging old ladies!

Involvement in cases won ended for me at the point the case was decided, but not so this lost case, albeit it was the only one I lost.

For a start expenses, i.e. lost earnings and petrol money, can only be claimed from the Tribunal for cases won. Thus I had no expenses – out of pocket for three hours off work and petrol to Coventry and back before you add the £3 donated to feed him. On top of that, just about every Sunday night for the next three months or so he rang up wanting to borrow a couple of quid until his Giro cheque came because he 'really, really liked' me! I was left wondering which sex his 'girlfriend' was.

Turning down such requests, which were not unusual, did not bother me as such because there was no way I could give money away to an ever-increasing 'clientele' – I had learnt that much in the Army. However, such phone calls did have a worrying aspect, besides the disruption to my family life on Sunday evenings. How long before one such character decided to demand money by menaces? For example, as I made my way to a house call in the same high-rise block of flats, I could easily be cornered and threatened – or worse?

Headlines 'Councillor found stabbed' would get no sympathy whatsoever because everyone would automatically excuse themselves from the problem by saying, 'Old Hughie must have been up to no good to be in that car park at that time of night – he didn't even live anywhere near there.'

The need for such welfare-type of work by Councillors is greater than it should be owing to the incompetence of agencies, which should cover some if not all of these situations. Not being allowed access to the national phone at work and arriving home outside office hours necessitated writing to report constituents in need of help. Straight away there is the normal postal service delay. Worse still, replies would only be typed some two weeks later, however urgent the situation, and then only to say the situation 'would be looked into'. In practice that usually meant passing them to another agency – and another two weeks' delay at each stage and so forth.

Having experienced early on this two-to-three-week delay period (which constituents blamed on me) an immediate house call by me seemed much more helpful, hence our Ward Councillor's card stated 'Only a phone call away'.

However, some situations were even more urgent and obviously required professional help. For example, a workmate came up to me at work immediately I arrived at 7.30 a.m. and explained that he kept an eye on his very elderly man-and-wife neighbours. The wife was permanently bedridden and relied on the elderly husband, but that morning the old boy was too ill to get out of bed himself. Being black, my workmate was fearful of losing time at work or arriving late, thus he had reluctantly been unable (at 7 a.m.) to make any arrangements for them – no one would be manning offices before 9 a.m. anyway.

During 9.30 tea break I listed the details, marked the envelope 'Urgent – must action today', and fought for a Pass Out. I not only delivered it to the counter of the DHSS Welfare Department but further explained to the young lady the urgency of the situation – someone needed to be with the old couple within the hour, I insisted.

Two weeks later a letter arrived at my home. 'Thank you for your letter regarding Mr & Mrs ... I must apologise for the delay in replying but your letter was on my desk unopened when I returned from holiday this morning' – and so on and so forth. The old couple could have been dead and buried by that time.

I risked my job and promotion, ran around using my own petrol on top of losing wages – but the professionals? They have seen it all before, of course, and just shrug their shoulders, meanwhile counting the days to their next holiday. Any advice and help I could give had got to be better than that. Fortunately the meals-on-wheels lady had found the old couple in time to get help. Both had to be taken to hospital.

I will move on to other contacts with unemployed in similar circumstances to the man in the previous Tribunal case. Just how do they get balanced meals, I thought? Just about all my football team, including the Manager and the

Coach, were unemployed. I resolved to try to help them if I could.

Calling on several Greengrocers I discovered they dumped quite a lot of vegetables and fruit which became unsaleable but were not yet rotten. The produce had lost its freshness and spoilt the shop display, but was edible.

Fresh goods were bought in particularly on Friday mornings ready for weekend sales, thus I arranged to call after work on Thursdays and collect an estate-car boot full of saleable fruit and veg at grossly reduced rates. By arrangement I dropped them off at the football team Manager's house. In theory, the players, friends and families would call during the weekend, as most players would have to anyway, and collect set amounts of say 20p a time. I would take any leftover (too far gone) the following week and feed it to my backyard hens.

Cauliflowers, sprouts, carrots, apples, oranges, grapefruit, frying tomatoes and so on – it was a mountain of stuff, about 2 cwt in all. Of course it varied in quality and was a differing assortment from week to week. I did not think that would matter for hungry families – but it did!

Excuses, excuses, week after week.

'The cauliflowers had wilted leaves.' Who eats the leaves? 'The apples had bruised skins.' It's advisable to peel even fresh apples in case of spray residues!

'I found an orange with a rotten middle bit' – as you would expect one or two to have at about 20p for 28 lb of goods.

'The mushrooms were black' – what colour do fresh mushrooms go when cooked, pray?

'We bought bulk yesterday' was the final one that beat me.

Obviously they did not want to be treated as second-class citizens. In any event I was paying £2 per week, plus time and petrol, and never, ever saw a penny in return – nor any leftover goods for my hens either.

Charity has its limits I concluded, after about six weeks.

However, I did not wish to break the contacts with the Grocers, therefore I dropped the produce off at an unemployed Party member's home for use or redistribution as he saw fit. It had not moved by the following week and I got very strange looks to boot. The second-class citizen stigma was even more pronounced between equals within a Socialist group I decided and abandoned that idea, albeit he had six young children.

For a few weeks the goods stacked up at home despite my own taste by now for grapefruit, kiwi fruit, grapes, melons and so forth. Then a call came via the Party for any old furniture, bedding, sleeping bags or cooking utensils for the newly formed Peace Camps at USAF bases. Cooking utensils? Presumably they would need bulk food to cook in them. For several months it found its way via a local CND activist to the nearest Peace Camp, albeit I was standing the £2 per week myself in the name of 'the cause' this time.

With the first arrests my regular contact was locked up – the first of several misdirected incarcerations for the good lady. My weekly £2 seemed trivial by comparison now! However her family no longer needed to make the weekly trip to the Peace Camp – and I had the fruit and veg on my hands again.

The quantity had dropped considerably because Grocers had curtailed their buying on seeing how much was unsold each week. Removing it little by little on a daily basis did not give the same impression. However, one contact maintained a regular Thursday supply explaining, 'Your first loss is your best loss.' It kept his display fresh, it saved him a trip to dump it, he bought in less, and anyway he was pleased to get it used. He was disappointed when I explained my redistribution problems, but urged me to persist one way or another.

About this time I discovered via press items that two

close mates had daughters who needed a tremendous amount of hospital treatment owing to congenital bone structure problems. The specialist hospital units where their daughters spent half their lives were in neighbouring towns. The extras plus travel and special aids were heavy expenses – hence the press items featuring fundraising events by charitable organisations on their behalf. Another mate had three sons on, or between, training courses who were eating him out of house and home, which goes on despite their non-earning positions. Another had a grandchild allergic to milk and needing special diets; another was a single parent struggling to support a son through A levels with no grants available, not even unemployment benefit.

Thus it is that to this day I collect £2 worth of wilted fruit and veg, split the produce four ways and distribute three parts to regulars and one where the need is most pressing. My workmates do not object to paying me 50p for a big box of assorted (non-) fresh fruit and veg. Perhaps it is because I slip in any surplus eggs from my hens, pot plants from my greenhouse, and never-ending bunches of sweet peas or dahlias when in season. I call it my 'food co-op' and threaten to pay a divi when they offer more than 50p.

Mentioning backyard hens brings me on to a failure item during my years as a District Councillor, but it had a very funny side to it, plus educational sidelines as originally intended.

One of the dreams I nurtured while a School Governor was to encourage a back-to-nature line of studies. I suppose it would be called 'Rural Studies' in the academic world. I just thought of it as getting eight- to twelve-year-old children from urban estates, and high-rise blocks in particular, into contact with Mother Nature – my allotmenting instincts coming out I suppose. Thus they would appreciate the beauty of, and need for, basics such as meadow grasses, clovers, meadow flowers, even weeds, as cover for creepy crawly insects, which make such areas their home. From there, up the food chain to us. En route, understanding the need to be careful with fungicides and insecticides would widen the studies into the science world. Having established the link between us and such basics, it was my belief they would have a higher regard for, and interest in, simple things such as grassed areas, gardens, and eventually the countryside generally. Whole generations are now living in a pre-packed, graded, sell-by-date, piped, canned, instant world. Their chances of making it if they should be a survivor after the next, instant war are just about nil also. Once the (uncontaminated?) shelves are empty they will not know where to start to look for alternative sources of food and which wild plants are poisonous.

Schools did mark off a small area of playing fields to observe the survival of the fittest as grasses, weeds and clovers competed unattended – but it proved impossible to protect from 'progress'.

School playing fields are cut by visiting County Council staff on a regular basis. Such groundsmen had, no doubt, been disciplined over the years for missing odd corners. No way were they going to get the sack for missing a bit now, whatever this or that Head dashed out and told them. They had their instructions! Anyway, small marker pegs holding up bits of string mean nothing to mechanical mowers with a driver sitting aloft well out of the way of any splintered wood.

Ah well! After several years of trying, a mountain of letters to and from the school and the Education Office and stalwart teachers risking being chopped up with the grass, a few square yards finally survived.

Ideally with this natural area goes a pond, of course, but an old bath is all schools can run to these days. However, just leaving water to stand a while allows children to see it go green with algae – the initial food in the food chain. Even this is a new experience to them, living in a world of instant, filtered, purified, chlorified, high-pressure piped water. Soon they discover water spiders miraculously arrive and a host of wriggly black things, with any luck (perhaps a bit of help) frog spawn. Hey presto! They have created their own little world even if it did take six months where the Creator took only six days. This delay brings the scientific exploration of the Creation much more into focus and again the food chain, even evolution, become much more realistic to them. It does not all arrive via 'the man from the Council' or via the DHSS Giro cheque!

The obvious next step is to hatch chicks from eggs, especially now with 'bird nesting' banned, even if it were possible in urban areas. Hopefully such attractions might encourage the difficult child to attend school more regularly – at least while the chicks were about. Add a few tame mice and a rabbit (where not already kept) and nature unfolds before their very eyes – but you are in trouble with the School Caretaker who will not want the added burden of feeding livestock during school holidays.

It was with this latter point in mind, plus the difficulty of getting sitting hens and fertile eggs, that I made myself a chicken coop and run in the back garden. I bought some rare-breed hens of a sitting disposition at the Fur and Feather Show – White Silkies with the added advantage of being non-flying and very docile birds. Beautiful fluffy balls of silk in fact. They will walk around the garden with you like a pet dog and will live on house scraps in tune with their natural forest floor instincts. The originals are black for camouflage – the whites have been carefully bred as with the steel grey and golden varieties.

The white strain is easily visible, therefore the hens are easily observed from the kitchen window and immediately become a conversation subject. Before you know it the whole family is spending less time watching television and more time observing, talking about (and talking to) the hens, which leads to their discussing their family and personal problems, hopes, aspirations and the facts of life. With a bit of luck hens may even keep lonely people out of the nuthouse. They certainly encourage a more structured day at times of severe stress – someone has to get up to feed them.

All this I thought would lead to a Backyard Poultry Association so that advice, tips, sitting hens and fertile eggs could be interchanged. Certainly local schools could have a regular supply of sitting hens and fertile eggs plus somewhere to return growing broods and hens to cover school holiday periods.

Not so!

I had forgotten all about neighbours. In order to get fertile eggs you must have a cockerel, and cockerels crow and crow and crow and… especially in the mornings.

Ah well! At least I got the headlines again and my follow-up explaining letter got the educational/therapy side across to those who read it.

The cockerel news item caused great amusement and I was the toast of the show everywhere I went for a few months. I am still standing by with fertile eggs, having changed breeds to a less audible cockerel – plus adding a few more hens to keep him worn out and too shattered to crow in the mornings. It's a great life being a cockerel. I must remember to come back as one.

Moving on to another aspect of a Councillor's duties…

Knees-up on the Rates

It may be that my puritan outlook protects me from invitations to functions the press would have everyone believe are a main part of public service. I think not, because invitations are sent out by officers, on behalf of those in high office, by working down a list of elected members. They would have no idea of my likes and dislikes or that I was a lifelong teetotaller and non-smoker. However, my wife enjoyed the social chit-chat and the glamour of such occasions. The problem was, there just weren't any such functions of note and the few that there were were very formal indeed. These were not exactly 'knees-up on the rates' – if they were on the rates at all. Mayor's and Chairman's allowances are so meagre both office holders invariably have to pay for such functions out of their own pockets before their term is over.

At the Mayor's reception and again at the Chairman's reception, I would take a host's sherry and walk around with it so that I could put it to my lips for the toasts, particularly to toast the Queen. However, even if I had actually drunk it (two sherries per year), was that a 'knees-up on the rates?' I did not think so. These two occasions were all very boring and formal and cost me either a Saturday's morning overtime or a pleasant morning on my allotment. I was only there representing my constituents, not for the beer. They were not functions I attend normally although I am still invited as an ex-Councillor.

At the end of the Mayor's year of office a customary dinner was given for invited guests including all District Councillors within the town's boundary. It was his or her 'thank you' parting function, of course. This was the only function that could possibly be described as approaching a 'knees-up on the rates', but in practice was a very subdued, formal, overdressed occasion and coming at the end of his/her year was more than likely paid for out of personal income – their allowance long since having been spent.

The Chairman's Charity evening, on the other hand, cost £8.50 per head. No one ever wanted to buy my ticket off me – yet they still complained it was a 'knees-up on the rates'.

These functions, for whatever reason, were all pleasant enough of course in a rather formal way, but we were all busy people and we were not there for the beer. Indeed after the first host's sherry all other drinks had to be bought, so where did the knees-up on the rates come in? It was not part of my lifestyle before being elected, nor is it now. I was only there representing my constituents, supporting their Mayor or their Chairman, officers who in turn were representative of their Queen and their Government respectively.

To illustrate this point further (because no one will believe the above résumé), I will itemise my one and only attendance at a dinner to celebrate the election of a Mayor in my first year of office. It was a word-of-mouth invitation, 'Don't forget the dinner [lunch] afterwards' approach. Thus my wife and I drifted over to the hotel with colleague Councillors and took our seats at the luncheon table, carefully minding our Ps and Qs in such a posh hotel, way above our usual lifestyle. Dinner was served and we enjoyed the main course even if it was a bit ordinary – potatoes and mash-type. Nevertheless, this is the life from now on we thought. Why worry, the rate-payers are forking out. Rock on, Tommy!

Before the sweet was served, up jumped a Councillor on the top table and announced that he was not a wealthy man, therefore, would we all pass up pronto £3.50 per head for the dinner he had had to pay for in advance (1976 prices).

Seven quid for potatoes and mash we could have had at home for seven shillings – plus a snatch of Saturday sport on the telly thrown in!

'Knees-up on the rates' be damned. I never had any and I did not go to celebrate the Mayor's election again either. Newly elected Mayors do have a heavy year's programme ahead of them but they do not need me to eat an expensive self-paid-for dinner to set them off on it.

However, the lack of any social occasions causes a problem for busy Councillors, in my opinion. Just how do such Councillors collectively say thank you to their spouses for all the behind-the-scenes work, telephone answering, typing, and holding the fort at home they do while we are out attending to constituents' problems? We are at meetings ensuring others can enjoy quiet evenings at home confident that all the services they will use the next day (including clean air to breathe) is laid on for them. Spouses can get somewhat fed up and not a little annoyed when deserted night after night, week in week out, month after month for years on end while house repairs, car maintenance and children go unattended. It's a problem that the public never considers. I know because I was one such member of the public right up to the time of my election.

I have pointed out that these functions were pretty formal – not exactly occasions at which you would let your hair down, perhaps because we were unused to the settings. This was a problem for me even at Council meetings where the array of formal dark suits tended to be a bit overpowering. Town Halls are, in the normal course of events, places the working man enters cap in hand – holy ground as it were. I suppose my downcast demeanour and subsequent attitude showed, because at my Swearing In the Chief Executive read the riot act to me as well, telling me he did not want to read in the press issues that had not been dealt with in Council. He laid it on pretty thick along these lines, leaving me in no doubt who was the boss. I did the working-man act mumbling, 'yes, sir, no, sir' type replies and left feeling totally deflated just two days after coming top of the poll in my Ward. It left me feeling that the election had been a paper exercise only in the Chief Executive's world. He had been, and still was, the boss, even if elected faces changed from time to time.

This 'I'm in charge' act was repeated over the next few weeks each time I bounced into Heads of Council Departments – with one exception. I got very despondent at one stage, to the extent of having to be talked out of resigning. Stand up and fight was the advice of my colleagues – mainly academics who had not suffered this browbeating, of course. They were acceptable to fellow clerics!

As the sheer weight of constituents' inquiries hit me and pointed to a ten-, fifteen-, even a twenty-one-year delay in officer's service plus indications of incompetence, I took courage.

I certainly could not make matters worse so I threatened them with the Ombudsman (in writing) and everything changed. Our roles reversed after about six months. As previously stated, I had good service – with the possible exception of the Planning and Technical Department where top officers had to be replaced eventually and replaced again before my time was up. However, I never did quite master the Town Hall building's overawing effect, even after mastering the officers.

I have earlier pointed out that at work I needed a Pass Out to leave the premises in order to get past the Police Lodge. Police Lodges had to be passed when arriving and leaving anyway – which tends to subdue one somewhat. Passes are also required to move inter-Division within the factory, for example to Wages/Personnel Departments or to an external telephone point (Police Lodge in practice). Even then there were separate Canteens, Personnel Offices, and so forth for staff and Manual employees. On top of this, even within a division a working man is labelled with different coloured overalls and subject to discipline if off his section without good reason, plus, of course, there are separate toilets for staff and Manual employees. The reader will deduce by now that to be caught using (say) an Office telephone, or in a Front Office, or even in the corridors leading to the Front Offices without a Pass and a good reason would mean instant dismissal – and has done so.

Thus even at work, while attending an interview for whatever reason, a worker is wrong-footed, uncomfortable and invariably dries up saying very little. He is off his muck heap and, therefore, feels stranded, unprotected, as it were. Only after the interview and when he is back among mates will he kick himself for not speaking up, asking questions, putting his side over, as the case may be.

There are very distinct dangers in speaking up if it's a disciplinary hearing when the pressures are applied even more – hence I was refused permission to return to the Shop Floor when asked to wait two hours during my Pass Out discipline. I even had to ask permission to use the staff-only toilet during this period (you will agree to anything after such treatment). Over the years I have been ordered out of a staff toilet although only using the nearest one when in 'civvies' on a week's internal course. I have been ordered out of a staff coach after missing the 7.15 a.m. daily Works bus leaving to take 'key' workers to set up a new factory twenty-two miles away in Banbury. While in the new factory I was ordered out of the staff 'canteen' which was only an office in temporary use with an imaginary line dividing staff and Works sections.

It is possible to get a bit nervous about posh places after a lifetime of this treatment, as most manual workers will affirm. I first encountered it as a Private in the Army, of course.

This same effect bore down on me in the Town Hall. Council Chamber meetings were even worse because there were the other fifty-seven Councillors now acting as 'interviewers', plus a row of Chief Officers, who kept their eyes glued on you throughout any speeches. I never even got used to entering the toilet marked 'COUNCILLORS'. It did not say which sex, still less whether staff or Manual. I found it most uncomfortable in a guilty way to be in there and was always expecting to be ordered out. For that matter, I was not too happy in the corridors either – wide, high and dominating. Formal suits and opening prayers wrong-footed me at first also, along with large, polished tables and matching chairs.

When you add the Chief Officer's 'do-as-I-say' opening acts and then finding a Controlling Group outnumbering you three to one all ready to jeer and interject smart-alec comments if you drop a word or use a wrong adjective, it's little wonder some new Councillors take years to make their maiden speech. One or two seldom turned up after the first few weeks of intimidation of one sort and another. Some such Councillors were experienced Trade Union men, holding prominent Union Office, yet the change from the question and answer informal Union proceedings to making speeches ranging over the whole issue under debate, at points in a debate only when called (perhaps five or six speeches after indicating) only to hear their points ridiculed later without further opportunity to reply, broke even such established Union men. One such colleague never spoke during his four years in office and declined to stand again, and one walked out when ridiculed halfway through his maiden speech and we seldom saw him again or heard from him either, nor did he stand again – yet he was a well-respected Union Convenor in 'real' life.

It's easy to see why steps were taken to control both Trade Unions and Labour Councils in Parliament – remove these two training grounds and the manual worker is voiceless and, therefore, completely controllable without applying any visible controls.

Another aspect of politics, which may or may not be expected of a District Councillor, is taking part in, or organising demonstrations both locally or on a wider scale.

I had been an ardent demonstrator on national issues ever since representing the factory's Shop Steward's Committee at the London demonstration in 1971 protesting against the Ted Heath anti-union bill. I continued joining such London demonstrations protesting against nuclear missiles, nuclear power, The Cuts, and more anti-Trade Union Bills. In between, 'March for Jobs' demos had taken my wife and me to all points north and south as well. Even before being elected to the Council I had filled the Public Gallery with allotmentors, protesting about a five-fold increase in rents. I had come to realise the effectiveness of a well-organised demonstration – complete with banners and slogans to make the point and keep spirits up.

On being elected Councillor, a number of parents, football organisers and sports club leaders in my Ward approached me pointing out the need for a hardcore kicking area on the park within the estate. This park had been landscaped at its inception in contours to prevent football playing. A 3,000-dwelling council estate without a football playing area? Planners are crazy people – but Councillors of the day must have passed it. I got the blame because constituents immediately attach to their Councillor an ongoing tag. To them you are a link in a continuous chain of incompetent, inconsiderate buffoons. I just happened to be a link they could actually approach at work, on the allotments, in the car park, in the streets, wherever, they had no inhibitions about giving 'old Hughie' an earbashing, in language of their choice too. I have already indicated that it is not possible to get a lifetime of pent-up feelings off your chest if your Councillor is a Solicitor, Estate Agent, School Teacher, professional or businessman and you are expected to say it all on their territory on their terms, but I was in my constituents' backyard, and no such inhibitions existed in my case.

Thus it was that I formed a Sports Action Group to press for a hardcore kicking area. In turn this group and its supporters filled the Public Gallery too.

The hardcore area never materialised. Face-to-face meetings with the Chairman of the Amenities/Recreation Committee and his Chief Officer spiked their guns. Carefully prepared for and prolonged 6 p.m. meetings soon wore the Action Group down – in particular by putting the onus on them to find the supposed £40,000 for the area. They dwindled away leaving me the sole negotiator with no pressure group to force home their points.

I learnt from this experience that I should have protected inexperienced people – mostly young parents with family pressures – from the professionals. I should have been the front man in Council and used them as shock troops only. Their case was lost by default, as it were. Still, one must live and learn – that's the name of the overall game.

Over the years I had a multitude of tenants complaining about the damp and mouldy conditions of their flats. Always the Housing Officer's reply was, 'Condensation – needs adequate heat and ventilation.' Tenants' electricity bills (their only form of heating) were enormous and still conditions deteriorated. I took every opportunity to speak on the subject in Council, but as I was not on the Housing Committee it was difficult to find pegs to hang speeches on. There is never AOB on District Council Meeting Agendas. Then the Tenants Association worked up a head of steam over the problem – plus noise between flats (enough to cause embarrassment), leaking roofs, poorly insulated lofts and numerous other items of complaint. They asked me to attend their meetings. In fact, they would not hold a meeting without me and arranged them to suit my availability. I also received numerous phone calls asking for guidance in between. This time I kept myself in an advisory capacity only and avoided the mistake of becoming part of a team. Tenants' representatives did again meet Housing Committee Officers and members at meetings pressed for by me. They quickly got disillusioned also. But now they could turn to me for advice again. I had not been knocked out with the team and felt free to suggest other avenues – meanwhile keeping up the pressure in Council and thus in the press.

A rent strike was thought to be a last resort. Despite my repeated pushing, tenants made no attempt at writing letters to the press either, therefore no pressure and embarrassment could be brought to bear via that channel. The face-to-face meetings had killed their enthusiasm for any more banner-waving gallery scenes. It's not easy when both sides recognise one another.

It so happened that the Chairman of the Housing Committee lived in the Ward, but represented another Tory Ward, of course. One of the tenants' main complaints was the otherwise perfectly good clothes that had to be thrown away once they got the stench of the 'condensation' mould on them. Friends would comment on the 'funny smell' when they wore them. I suggested they should have a mass throw away one Sunday afternoon and throw them into the front garden of the Housing Chairman's house. The press would conveniently be passing, of course.

The result was magic – even if the Chairman did not take too kindly to the method used!

Central heating was extended into bedrooms, roof leaks were stopped, lofts were re-insulated, cavity walls were filled, ceiling to neighbour's floor above interchanges were reinforced and filled with sand to cut down noise transmissions – £10,000 per flat was found and the work done pronto, when one £5,000–£10,000 kicking area had been talked out via dubious sums described as getting the Sports Action Group to 'see the real problem'.

Standing a little way back behind the pressure group had brought results and always left me free to speak on the subject in Council by way of inquiring the current position – as if I didn't already know.

Subsequently I advised even allotment associations in this way. I also got a one-and-a-half-page thank-you letter from an anglers association without even speaking in Council on their problems.

A lot is being said in Party meetings these days about 'Women's Causes' without ever identifying them. I confess I do not understand the phrase – or do not go along with it, perhaps. I take up issues and assist groups and if some of these issues are particular to women, then so be it. If the cause is right then I will endeavour to help without stepping on the toes of other people or sections of the community if possible.

Thus it was that when only the women, mostly young girls, went on strike for Union recognition at a local factory, I immediately threw my lot in with them. Nevertheless, I was frequently one of only three or four men who kept in regular daily touch with the striking girls over the ten-week strike. The others were husbands or boyfriends; full-time Trade Union Officials turned up at intervals, of course.

Each dinner hour I dropped off placards I had made for them and collected them on the way home at night. They enjoyed learning little 'revolutionary' ditties, for example 'Build a Bonfire' with suitably named people they wished to burn on top and in the middle. Changing words to other well-known tunes kept their spirits up also.

It was a warm spell and a singing break went well between sunbathing on the pavements outside a factory.

However, the time came when they wanted more action. The ditties went very well as we marched down Leamington's Parade, my banners aloft, on a Saturday morning, with a number of parents and families joining in behind the AUEW's huge banner.

A good time was had by all. The girls won union recognition, but they are still having it hard at work. Rome was not built in a day, I fear.

In between such local events my wife and I still made regular trips to demos in London – and all points north, east and west should the occasion arise. I had always enjoyed such marches both for a good cause and to get rid of pent-up inhibitions by 'legally' walking down some of the most famous streets in Britain shouting catchphrases at all and sundry – and singing!

As a long-standing Male Voice Choir Singer I had thought I was good at it – however the Cardiff 'March for Jobs' demo lifted my singing to new heights. Why don't we have more demos in Cardiff?

There are demonstrations and demonstrations. I started with a huge London one (150,000 strong) and worked down via local small factory demos to advising filling the Public Gallery. But it is possible to demonstrate on a one-man scale to make a point otherwise being ignored.

I have pointed out the one to three minority position of the Labour Group of Councillors in Council. Obviously we lost every vote, but democracy is about debate and the right to put your point over. Given that right you battle on hoping that one day your arguments will affect the ballot box results and swing the balance in your favour. Suppress the right to debate and democracy has gone out through the window. Refuse this point and minority groups are left to make their point in whatever way they can because the hope of affecting the ballot box result has been denied them.

On the other hand a controlling group (and it happens elsewhere where Labour is the controlling group) find lengthy debates a bit of a waste of time because their built-in majority dictates the result before the debate even starts. They are all busy people and sitting in Council listening to speech after speech which will in no way affect the result pre-decided along Party lines can be a bit boring – especially when they have heard all the arguments plenty of times before at every cycle of the Council meetings on some subjects.

Housing debates, for example, went on and on. All Labour Councillors were prepared to partake and Liberals tried to keep their end up also. However, the controlling Tories had little interest in housing and this was reflected in debate. They had only two main speakers on the subject and a few others only willing to try short comments – none really wanted to take part. Against this all twelve Labour Councillors were raring to go, hands aloft and half out of their chairs as a previous speaker took his seat. A chance to get on to the Housing Committee was also at stake – a good speech and the next Committee reshuffle might get you there.

Thus it was that successive housing debates in full council were cut short immediately their two main housing speakers had got in, by Tories moving 'Next Business'. This curtailing of debates, the housing debates in particular, made us mad. It was our main manifesto plank – more council houses, more OAP dwellings, more sheltered and very sheltered units, better and quicker repairs, stabilised rents, expanded housing Direct Labour Force – speakers were clued up with latest statistics, waiting lists numbers obtained that very day from Housing Officers, transfers wanted, young families in distress, children in high-rise blocks, examples of actual constituency cases to quote, headline in the next day's papers to get to prove to constituents you were there fighting. Bang! 'Move next business.' Carried. Wham! Prepared speeches, memorised speeches, maiden speeches – all shut off and every Tory is now jumping up and speaking at length on 'Lavatories for Dogs' or 'Improved Toilet Facilities for the All England Ladies Bowling Competition.'

At Labour Group Meetings our frustrations got vented, alternatives discussed and action plans drawn up to put a stop to this guillotining. Not only were democratic rights being denied us but our constituents were being denied a voice and access to our opinions on major issues. No debate – no press reports. Curtailed debates – curtailed press reports. Major housing debates came round only once per year when the Council's targets were set for the next year. It was our annual big chance and we were being denied it year after year.

During my first term of office an impromptu protest had been made by a colleague – our Shadow Housing Chairman – who got to his feet and attempted to make his speech even after 'Next Business' had been moved. The Council Chairman had adjourned the proceedings for ten minutes to get round the situation but still no debate took place.

This was again a possibility open to us but could not be used too often for fear of alienating the public if the press reported it as fits of temper. Anyway, who would now have the nerve? That colleague had been serving his last few months as a Councillor: he had not stood again owing to ill health. Three Labour colleagues died sudden deaths in office during my seven years' service. It's not an easy life.

After much discussion the Group decided on a Mass Walkout if 'Next Business' cut our big occasion down to two or three speeches only i.e. two from the Tories and only one from Labour.

This we did and it did get the press – story and editorial

– but it did not get us any more debate on housing or on anything else because we were not in the council chambers after that point.

The following year we decided that this tactic was not ideal and could leave us open on other issues raised after we left. Also housing comes up in two or three places in a Council Summons (Agenda). Although stopped when speaking in the appropriate place we normally attempted to continue the curtailed debate as each subsequent housing item was called. This we could not do after a mass walkout. Also all other issues went through by default, as it were, since we were not present to debate them. Mass walkouts were clearly not on; besides, the shock effect had now been used as well. For all we knew the Tories would plan to add, via amendments, some quite controversial items once we had left the chamber.

So what could we do to press our right to debate?

You guessed it. I was chosen as the one with sufficient nerve to jump up and shout, I do mean shout, arguments until the Chairman adjourned the meeting. Our protest would be made. The press were alerted to our feelings and we could return to the Chambers to get speeches in under the adjourned subject and subsequent housing items, if possible. Hopefully the Controlling Group would recognise our right of debate and stop moving Next Business in the future.

We would, of course, debate other issues as they came up and be present to highlight and block any crafty additions being added as Amendments along the way.

On the night (two nights later in practice), I did as planned – got on my feet immediately 'Next Business' had been moved and before it could be passed, then commenced my housing speech. Of course, the Chairman attempted to out-shout me with, 'Sit down Councillor Griffiths.' I had to out-shout him and doing this did not allow checking with prepared notes – a glance down would denote defeat in the shouting match. I had had plenty of practice at work when trying to get a Pass Out. Thus I found myself repeating the first three minutes or so of the speech with ever-increasing vehemence. Christ, the Chairman that night was hard to push but eventually he adjourned. He subsequently explained to me he did not realise it was a Group tactic and thought I would burn myself out – hence the long delay as it appeared to me.

Outside in the corridor where I was, of course, perfectly normal and in no temper as everyone thought, word soon got around it was a Group tactic and the Chairman called us back in after only a few minutes. The Tory Group Leader made a statement to the effect he now knew I was under Group orders and, therefore, he was prepared to continue without further reference to my behaviour. This the council did and housing was debated at length. On subsequent issues I was called and spoke and my points were taken seriously – no one making jokes or capital out of my earlier disruptive behaviour at the Council meeting. Nor did it come up at subsequent meetings.

We subsequently had one year of long, uninterrupted housing debates. However, the Labour Party (my Branch) was to kick me out and let three Tories in via my Ward at the end of that term of office.

You cannot win them all, however hard you try.

Try for Parliament

As a regular reader of the *Labour Weekly*, I noticed the item announcing Parliamentary Selection dates on which Constituencies would select their Candidate. Constituency Secretary's names and addresses were given inviting interested people to send their personal details. As the 1979 elected Government began to run out of time in office the list of places announcing selection dates grew longer and moved southwards from the Labour strongholds in the North. Also, as selections were completed the candidates chosen began to broaden and move away from sitting MPs or ex-MPs and displaced MPs by boundary changes, to manual workers and variation of same. Academics, barristers and solicitors were thinning out in the successful Candidates' ranks listed weekly. On top of this articles appeared arguing the need for more manual workers to come forwards. Many more articles appeared arguing the need for women – but I didn't feel a sex change coming on. When the neighbouring Constituency of Rugby asked for applications to send personal details I decided to have a go. It would be an experience and, Rugby being near, neither travelling expenses nor time spent would cripple me.

This initial application was short-lived but it started me on a long run, which took my wife and me all over the Midlands from Leicester down to Stroud – twenty-one such trips in fact. It was an experience all right, and one we thoroughly enjoyed. The warm welcomes and attentive Branch meetings were followed in four cases by equally packed and attentive Constituency meetings for the final selection. Such appreciation lifted both of us onto a new plateau. It gave a sort of stamp of approval to the (then) six and a half years of slogging Ward work and the grind of Council work generally. At no time did either of us lose any time off work to get to meetings. We drove to evening Branch meetings after work and made it back by 1 a.m. or so. Constituency meetings were held on Saturdays where I was shortlisted. Of course, at least one previous Saturday afternoon had to be spent in the area to get the layout (factories, housing estates, main town/village locations) and to buy some local newspapers to find out any pressing local issues that were likely to come up in question time. Yes, we enjoyed these occasions. It's amazing what you can see in a place when you have a reason for looking.

Unfortunately, as it turned out, it tempted me into entering the race in my own Constituency. Alas, a prophet is without honour in his own country, or so the Good Book tells me. And so it proved. Also, I never rose to the occasion locally – no forceful up-and-at-'em-boys speeches. I presumed everyone knew me and of my wide-ranging activities from the many press items covering the same over the years. Anyway I was not known locally for forceful speeches in Party Meetings (and Party members are not at Council Meetings). I reasoned it was not the time to change styles for home consumption.

My local campaign was entirely based on horses for courses, as proved by fan mail, press coverage, top of the poll District results in my Labour-held Ward and a massive 991 votes when I stood for the county in a Tory Ward where Labour's best previous result had been 250. Pointing also to three Union Branch nominations (where other local Candidates had none) I argued this local support would carry me through without a high-powered campaign. Indeed, I reasoned to myself that such a local character was more likely to unseat a sitting complacent Tory MP rather than a mud-stirring newcomer.

I reasoned wrongly apparently, because an unemployed candidate swept through on the first ballot (over 51% for him against the other four of us put together).

The local Party had become introverted, loaded with unemployed, many of whom had not even got two years in the Party but were given General Management Committee delegates' posts because of the time they had to attend to such matters, presumably. They not only did not know me (i.e., really know me) but mistrusted all old-timers en bloc. After all, we had allowed Maggie to come to power in 1979, an act which had resulted in their current unemployed plight. We were a 'no good, do nothing' lot and 'sick and defeated past Party activists', to quote but two résumés I had to endure in GMC meetings.

Their man went on to come third in a two-horse race – a position not even a future better-known Candidate will pull back from in a hurry! The Tories were delighted with the choice, walking the course without a worry even after a large chunk of Toryland had gone to Rugby under boundary changes.

I had returned a day early from holiday to attend the Selection Conference held on a Sunday afternoon. The next evening my own Branch selected their three Ward Candidates. My failure the day before was well known by then, of course, especially since I had carried the Branch shortlisting. But when you are a loser, you sure are a loser. I failed to gain even one of the three District nominations for the Ward.

The Ward went on to lose all three seats to the Tories including my 600 majority. That vote had been nearly twice that of the nearest Tory and on the very day Maggie was elected in 1979. Effectively that Ward Selection Meeting had voted the Tories in and sent my six and a half years' hard slog down the drain.

Subsequently statistics show the Ward had the largest

swing against Labour in the whole of the British Isles – the Ward voters putting two fingers up at the replacements the Branch had chosen – according to the Constituency Secretary when contacted by Labour's London HQ for an explanation. Either way at least I got into Labour's record books.

My horses-for-courses approach was the right one but new Labour colleagues did not believe me. They were green and thought they could do it by force of right-sounding arguments, sweeping all before them and showing us old-timers how it's done to boot. They probably know better now – but where are they?

However, the Party will survive it all. I, with like-minded stalwarts, will still be around to pick up the pieces from time to time. Also, even out of these new factions a few more stalwarts will surface to take over when eventually I make the final selection meeting in a wooden overcoat.

Fan Mail

A trickle of appreciative letters from constituents or their families continued throughout my seven years' Council service. Not many, but they were very welcome to help me over low points when the non-stop abuse and criticism started to get through to me and my wife. 'So you are one of our idle Councillors' would be an initial approach at work by someone with a problem – not only expecting me to have the wit and experience to help, but ignoring the obvious, that I worked alongside them all day and was still expected to find time to sort their problems out. A thank you now and again used to help.

The high points were the deluge of letters to the press defending me when some ill-informed person wrote in attacking me. Even so there were a few surprises along the way. A mother wrote from Scotland thanking me for my advice to her daughter and son-in-law which led to them getting a transfer from a flat to a house. The advice was not such that I could commit to print, but it worked, hence the thank you letter from Scotland.

Soon after my becoming the Council's representative on the Marriage Guidance Council – not a body tailor-made to suit working-class Trade Union methods – a letter arrived from The Beeches in a area where you cannot get near the front door for horse boxes. The address plus the sender's position left me a bit perplexed.

Christ! My stay on the MG Council is going to be short, I thought as I started to read it.

Not so.

She had noted my forthright, pull-your-finger-out

approach over raising funds and she had also noted the shocked expressions on her colleagues' faces – but she hoped I would not lose heart. I was just what the MG needed an '...honest, straightforward approach...' – it went on and on. Just a Trade Unionist doing and playing their normal role, as I saw it.

You can never tell. It's surprising how many 'to-the-Manor-born' people regret having missed a working-class spell in their lives. Hugh Gaitskell of Labour Party Leadership fame was just such a person. My MG fan may be a secret Labour Party supporter even. In any event she still keeps telling me, 'You are the best thing that ever happened to us.' At fifty-three my knees still go all wobbly. Shucks!

Another thank-you letter I did not expect came from the local Angling Association. I have never held a fishing rod in my hand, thus the letter could not be on account of my fishing skills and, therefore, gave me quite a kick.

The initial contact was via a circular letter to all fifty-eight District Councillors, pointing out their difficulties in obtaining suitable river lengths. It was from outside my Ward – the opposite side of town, in fact.

Now there must be anglers or fishermen of sorts among fifty-eight Councillors as at that time it was the fastest growing sport with the greatest number of participants. However, apparently I was the one to offer advice.

At first they found my advice too hard to swallow but it so happened one of their Committee men was a mate at work and after prolonged discussions he told them to heed me. They came back for more. It would appear my reply and follow-ups brought satisfaction if a one-and-a-half-page thank you is a measure. As an outsider I saw their problem as a lack of communications – they needed to open and cultivate channels instead of feeling slighted owing to events of yesteryear which were of no account to current Council Officers. I suppose even dedicated League football managers must get into this frame of mind and, after years of hard slog, get the sack because they cannot see the trees for the wood, or what ever.

Another letter – perhaps not a 'fan mail' letter as such but nevertheless one that produced an inner glow – arrived after I had been knocked out of office. It was from a one-time leading member of the Controlling Group – a Tory! No wonder the Labour Party did not reselect me!

There is good and bad on all sides, of course, but this member had made it his business, in my opinion, to attack me and attach some stigma on me because of my known Trade Union activities. Thus during my early years any reference I made in Council about rent levels, electric, gas or water bills being too high and causing hardship to the underprivileged, were always attacked by him as due to Trade Unions 'such as the one Councillor Griffiths belongs to' forcing up prices – according to him. Nearly all Conservative Members belonged to Trade Unions or associations of a similar character. Some belonged to the AUEW like myself. However, apparently I was the focal point of such supposed Union-made problems, as he interpreted it.

I never bit and gradually such comments in Council sounded more and more pathetic and finally died. He himself became a 'backbencher' as the anti-Thatcherite Group took over and ousted him from a Committee Chairmanship (Maggie had a very low poll rating in 1980–81). Finally, as if from a lone voice crying in the wilderness, I got quite a cosy letter regretting my demise.

'Politics,' he wrote, 'is unfair, even evil at times.' He should know, he made me suffer in my early years as a Councillor. Although in fairness to him I have to say his comments were short and always in debate. Also he remains a Town, District and County Councillor, while I languish at home rejected. Such are the fortunes of a Socialist in a Shire County and in Royal Leamington Spa to boot.

I often wonder if Labour Party members in strong Labour heartlands such as the Metropolitan areas would be so forthright if they were up against three to one adverse majorities year in year out. Biting your tongue may come hard to them, some may even have jacked it in when they found they not only lost every vote on every issue but had to suffer criticism every time they spoke.

It can get you down, so the letter came as a fillip if a little belatedly.

The letters that recharged my batteries when taking such a battering were the short, carefully written – in almost childish style – letters from young parents thanking me for help. Of course, they were few, very few, in comparison to the two to four cases per week I averaged needing written memo work – probably as many again advised verbally, face to face, or on the telephone. Looking back I wonder, 'Are such problems being picked up now?' The Ward went Tory, hence Labour Councillor manned car parks and Indoor Surgeries ceased in 1983. Some school and house-buying problems I still advise at work but I cannot help even workmates if they have housing-repair problems, or need a council dwelling or a transfer.

Some would argue, 'So what? For every one you helped another was pushed back in the queue.' That point of view does not stop the ache in my heart.

All is not lost, however. As Chairman of the Youth Centre (next door to both car park and Indoor Community Centre Surgery points) I have encouraged and widened the activities to include advice giving. The Manpower Services Commission has helped by attaching a worker or workers following one another on twelve-monthly appointments. Thus the Youth Centre doors are open all day with unemployed 'Open House' club, a Toddlers Club (cover for Single Parents Club), and a Claimants and Welfare Rights afternoon.

You will not meet me there because I am at work, no longer being hounded by Foremen, but you will find the right spirit there. I like to think its mine.

Printed in Great Britain
by Amazon